KISSING THE DRAGON

KISSING

THE DRAGON

The Intelligent Work-Hunter's Companion

Madeleine Pelner Cosman, Ph.D.

BARD
HALL

Bard Hall Press
Tenafly, New Jersey

Designed by Janet Czarnetzki

Library of Congress Cataloging in Publication Data

Cosman, Madeleine Pelner
   Kissing the Dragon.

1. Professions—Vocational Guidance.   I. Title.

84-71095   1984

ISBN 0-916491-07-2

BARD HALL PRESS
32 Knickerbocker Road, Tenafly, New Jersey 07670

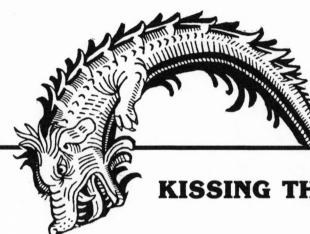

KISSING THE DRAGON

BARD

Truest Compassion in Greatest Strength

How *Kissing the Dragon* Came to Be

Millions of dollars in grants are as much a peril as a pleasure. As the founder and director of the Institute for Medieval and Renaissance Studies, City College of City University of New York, I have been raising such sums since 1969 for an academic enterprise consisting of 15 collaborating departments, 254 courses, and their associated professors, students, and staff. Though from the beginning I have insisted that every academic appointee and every undergraduate and graduate student understand that few could achieve permanent tenure, I quickly discovered that no one believed me. Marvelously intelligent men and women signing three year contracts nevertheless were shocked and dismayed when, two and a half years later, I could not guarantee a lifetime academic association. Excellent and otherwise realistic students whose fellowships ended seemed similarly surprised.

Probably I could have said, "What did you expect?" to my brilliant graduate students. I could have said, "Tough!" and closed the door on my colleague, soon to be jobless, with a son in college, two daughters in high school, and a recently handicapped wife. I elected instead to try rotating opportunity out of adversity. Together with these unemployed medievalists, I created a new corporation called Historic Spectaculars, the Educational Entertainment Service. We present historically splendid, exuberant Medieval and Renaissance concerts, lectures, feasts, and festivals for universities, schools, libraries, hospitals, businesses, shopping centers, theaters, and television. Historic Spectaculars' triple purpose has been employing talented performers, expanding the public audience for historical subjects, and training academics for new theatrical applications of old learning. For these same faculty and students, I also began formulating the concept of ingenious packaging of talents and predilections for creating jobs: the discovery tests, the templating, the proposing, and the total philosophical and practical technique of *Kissing the Dragon.*

I did not predict what happened next.

- A professor ecstatically pleased with his new job thought "dragon-kissing" would benefit his 23 year old son with an "unsaleable" B.A. degree in marine biology.

- A mature graduate student introduced the concept to her 54 year old husband threatening suicide because his microbiology position in a pharmaceutical firm was reorganized out of existence.

- An anthropologist, aged 45, "burned out, dead-ended, totally demoralized" needed a clever career change, heard about the "dragon service" at a cocktail party, and came to my office as a "last resort."

- A young orthopedic surgeon forced out of practice by astronomically high malpractice insurance premiums, which made it impossible to charge patients low fees and still endure financially, wondered whether the technique would work for him.

So any week of the year, an observer might find an intelligent work-hunter with no relationship whatsoever to the Institute for Medieval and Renaissance Studies sitting in an antique rocking chair in my office, contemplatively working on the *Cape of Competence* test or writing a definition of *Boots of Restriction* and *Spurs of Incentive.* Furthermore, I have introduced *Kissing the Dragon* to large audiences of academic graduate programs, career and placement conferences, executive "outplacement" groups, women's "reentry to business" programs, career changers' meetings, teachers' unions, societies of professors, and international congresses of learned societies.

What started, then, as an informal survival technique for my staff and students, became a more universally applicable process, equally successful with intelligent scientists as with humanists, and applicable not only to Ph.D.s but M.A.s and B.A.s wishing to market their talents successfully.

Kissing the Dragon is for the intelligent underemployed, unemployed, and unhappily employed requiring creative change of profession.

Contents

I

Naked Truth

When I was young, I had an old dowager aunt named Justine. She was exceedingly wealthy, precise, and deaf. Whenever she heard vague unpleasantries, she turned off her hearing aid and retired into the mathematical precision of the Baroque music in her head.

Whenever Aunt Justine wished rigorous expression from her nieces and nephews, she turned down the volume of her hearing aid, insisting we say it loud and clear. It is very hard to shout a complex generality. It is even harder to do it politely. So Aunt Justine taught us brevity and exactitude. If we could not say it loudly and clearly enough, she turned her hearing aid off entirely. "Draw it!" she demanded. It is very hard to draw a vague idea or a pious hope or an ambiguous platitude. So Aunt Justine taught us the virtues of unmitigated, uncompromising, incontrovertible, concrete truth.

With her wide-brimmed black velvet hat and her very large hearing aid on her breast, Lady Justine—for that is what the rest of the world called her—would meet the challenge you and I now face: the ingenious packaging of talents and predilections for Ph.D.s. She would begin with benevolent insults.

There you are looking sexless and silly with only a gold-tasseled mortarboard on your head. You have a Ph.D. Now what? Who are you? Where are you? What are you? That picture of you is grim and bleak. It has no distinguishing features, no setting, no color.

Since doctors are trained to despise dismal voids, you

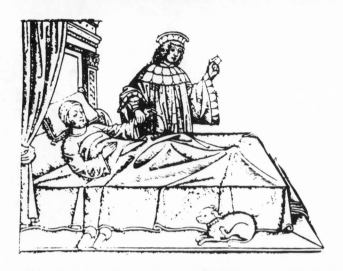

have to fill in the absent shapes, pigments, and designs. You answer that you are not a designer nor a painter but a Ph.D. in a serious subject. So sorry. There are no spare professional artists to paint your portrait. So you will have to do it. Anyway, no one else knows your true features so well as yourself.

Furthermore, you look a little sick. Doctor, heal thyself. You answer that you are not that kind of doctor. So sorry. Perhaps you have not heard. There is not a single healer interested in helping you now in your need. You are rather far gone. Why didn't you call at your first symptoms? Why have you intentionally smoked that academic weed so dangerous to your professional health? Why did you persevere in doing what could only lead to where you are?

Moreover, though I cannot see your eyes or ears, I notice your mouth has a slight downward curve on the left side. You think me sarcastic and cruel. Good professors told you that no matter how bad the academic job market, the best new Ph.D.s would find jobs. Since you believed yourself among the best, you were safe. You were arrogant. The professors were inaccurate. What they forgot to tell you, or perhaps you didn't hear, is that few available academic jobs now lead to tenure. The temporaries will leave you quite as underemployed in a few years as you are now.

"This is madness," you say. You did not ask to be scolded or sniped at. You want to stamp your foot and shout that excellent Anglo-Saxon epithet for excrement. But you are too polite a doctor to shout "Shit!" So you mutter it, and start to leave. So sorry. That is not possible. If you open the door you will see a fierce, foul, ferocious, fire-fuming dragon. It will not let you pass. There is no help.

You will simply have to paint yourself out of your corner.

You must rediscover talents and predilections you never forced yourself to acknowledge. Thanks to a set of clever nasty questions, you will garb yourself in something more than your gold-tasseled mortarboard.

Five fashionable garments fit Ph.D.s. First is the *Cape of Competence* which you will wear over your *Gown of Compatibility.* On your feet you will place the *Boots of Restriction* with their *Spurs of Incentive.* You will peer at the world through your *Spectacles of Suitability.* And beneath your mortarboard you will crown your head with a *Cap of Abstraction.*

Once clothed, you will have the courage to create a prospective position utilizing your doctoral training plus your other talents and predilections. Its purpose will be salary, current reward, and future hope.

II

Fashions for Philosophy Doctors

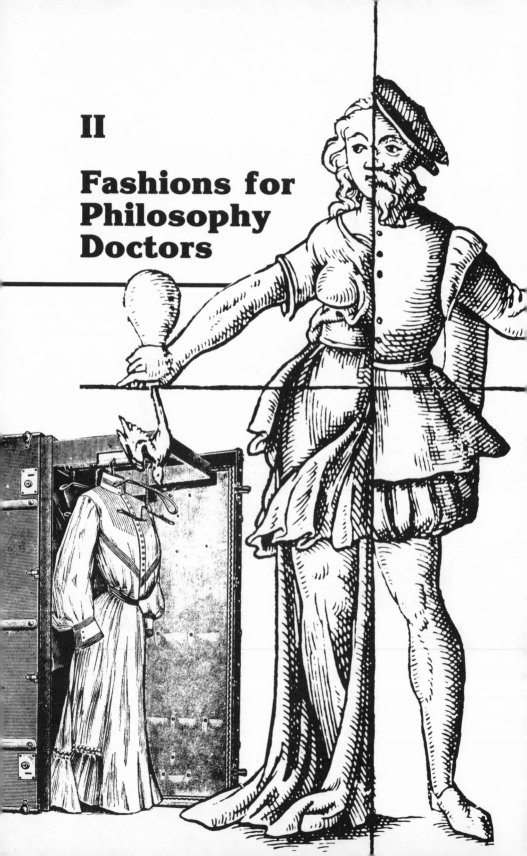

What in Heaven's name are these absurd-sounding garments?

Cape of Competence

is formed from the fabric of your talents, which are entirely separate from your doctoral training. In addition to your Ph.D. excellence, you may be an extremely competent pilot, stone mason, embroiderer, cataloguer, bicyclist, wine-taster, X-ray machinist, bartender, or copy editor. Good. You may never have thought of these as professionally useful in your future. Or you may think them incompatible with your Ph.D. Never mind. Perhaps you will reconsider later. That *Cape of Competence* will be worn over the

Gown of Compatibility

which is made from the cloth of your affinities to unlikely people and places. Your two types of expertise—first your Ph.D. training and, second, your other competences—may be beautifully compatible with children, medical centers, ships, telephone companies, zoos, or Bloomingdale's department stores. You may never have considered these but they are possibilities introduced by the

Boots of Restriction and Spurs of Incentive.

You have certain responsibilities and personal inhibitions keeping your feet firmly planted on your current turf. Cataclysmic events in your life restrict you, yet spur you on to particular actions or, at least, predilections and pre-judices: Divorce, illness, alcoholism, a friend's suicide; your surviving a crash, a fire, a war. Whether or not you are conscious of their control, such events bind you, limit you, push you, pull you. These appreciated humanely and creatively lead to the

Spectacles of Suitability

which perceive the best setting for your new profession. That may be rugged mountain country, a warm beach, a friendly small town, the city with seven airports, or the waves of the world's oceans. Locale may lead not only to personal pleasure but unguessed professional prospects, compatible with your (charming) peculiarities of personality revealed by the

Cap of Abstraction,

that skull cap under your mortarboard which reveals some of your emotional tolerances which you may not think praiseworthy, but now must admit. How strong is your love or your hatred for deadlines, mediocrity, red tape, liars, women, sweat, heavy drinkers, over-achievers, ostentation? While it might be nice to remake yourself or your unpleasant habits, the point now is to accurately assess the way these may serve to your advantage.

The five doctoral garments—*Cape of Competence, Gown of Compatibility, Boots of Restriction* and *Spurs of Incentive, Spectacles of Suitability,* and *Cap of Abstraction*—truly are discoverable only after you are introduced to the important, regal, imperious friend of Lady Justine. But before you meet her and before you think these ideas unrelated to you, here are four completely clothed Ph.D. portraits.

CASE 1
A Brilliant Ph.D. in Classical Languages

Cape of Competence (talents tested by experience and unrelated to Ph.D. specialty): animal training; department store window display; simplification of complex ideas.

Gown of Compatibility (capacity to use either Ph.D. specialty or competences with surprising audiences): animals, children.

Boots of Restriction and *Spurs of Incentive* (a cataclysmic event that affected life thereafter): watched, horrified, as his dog was tortured then shot by ignorant drunken teenagers.

Spectacles of Suitability (a passion for place): warm weather; beaches.

Cap of Abstraction (personal likes and dislikes): hates deadlines, condescension to children, pomposity.

JOB: Director of Education for the San Diego, California, Zoo. Prepares displays on real and fabulous beasts; lectures and writes popular articles on original Greek and Latin natural historical sources such as Pliny's *Natural History*, the *Physiologus*, and beast epics, as well as their relationships to modern nature.[*]

---

[*] All case histories throughout *Kissing the Dragon* are genuine, but specific names and details of jobs are disguised to protect the privacy of their holders. Please see the *Postscript*.

CASE 2
A Brilliant Ph.D. in History of Science

Cape: bicycling; private pilot; ordering closets; tinkering with antique aircraft.

Gown: libraries, medical personnel.

Boots and *Spurs:* spouse's severe kidney disease requiring intermittent dialysis, a long, expensive hospital procedure.

Spectacles: flat land for cycling; small cities with stable neighborhoods.

Cap: loves efficiency, command, meeting deadlines, intellectual and visual order.

JOB: Editorial Director of the Aerospace Medical Library, Wright State University Medical Center, Dayton, Ohio. Access to the original papers of the Wright Brothers, the history of aviation (as well as of cycling); fine flat terrain for bicycle and hostel trips; free medical care for self and family with good renal dialysis unit.

CASE 3
A Brilliant Ph.D. in Biochemistry

Cape: gourmet cooking; expertise with fine wine; civilized camping; fashion.

Gown: ships, wealthy people.

Boots and *Spurs:* financially and emotionally devastating divorce (wife left with lesbian lover).

Spectacles: elegant back-packing; peripatetic life with creature comforts.

Cap: loves changing work places; hates women.

JOB: Resident Program Director of gourmet world cruises for major international steamship company, serving cooking schools, gourmet food and wine groups, continuing professional education courses on shipboard in pharmacology, medicine, and business. Lectures on board and writes on biochemical actions of food and wine, and the biochemistry of health faddism.

CASE 4
A Brilliant Ph.D. in Comparative Linguistics

Cape: stone masonry; bricklaying; heavy construction machines.

Gown: old buildings; ruins; fragments of complete objects.

Boots and *Spurs:* survived bombing of home in Europe and loss of generations of family art and mementos.

Spectacles: tents, shifting locales.

Cap: hates repetitive predictability; loves daily challenge, sharpening skills, discovering one new thing each week.

JOB: epigrapher, interpreter, and translator of inscriptions on stones for urban rescue archaeology team of national historic preservation organization. Required to work in city excavations, wield trowel, drive a backhoe, and talk the language of unwilling construction workers angry their jobs in new construction must be delayed for saving "useless" remnants of the past. Team moves around country where needed.

Lady Justine garnered these garments for those four Ph.D.s with the help of a friend. On the chance you may never have met her, let me introduce the formidable, patrician, imperious, ingenious, philosophical noblewoman: Lady Rotation.

III

Rotation

Imagine a large spoked wheel suspended in the air. Place a throne at the top of the wheel, and seat a crowned figure on it. On the bottom rim of the wheel, place a pair of hands holding on for dear life. Attach a noble body with dangling legs. Now picture a tall, stern, regal woman at the left of the wheel. She is going to turn it. It is her wheel. We have no idea when she will spin the one on top of the world down to the depths, and raise the fortunes of the one below. As the wheel suddenly turns, off flies the throne and crown. The royal one must grab the wheel or be hurled into the abyss of unknowing. The patient rim-grabber below may soon rise to glory.

Lady Rotation often is mistakenly called Dame Fortune or Lady Chance or Lady Luck, the arbitrary spinner of human fate. But her real name, Rotation, means turning adversity into opportunity. She reminds people that nothing is necessarily forever. Every tribulation has hidden hope. After every dashed expectation there is possible new ascent to triumph. Evil can be turned to good. But the far side of distress is visible only to those first willing to see blatant ugliness on the wheel, and then imagine its radiant opposite. Glare makes most eyes turn away. But those bearing the brightness twice are devotees of Rotation forever.

This is the way Lady Rotation works.

You expect to drive forty miles for a job interview. Eagerly, briefcase in hand, you come out to the driveway and see your car with the left rear tire flat. You have two choices. The first: stamp the ground, kick the wheel, curse fate, beat your breast, raise your blood pressure, lament that the world is against you. Cry out in despair that you will never get there. Disconsolately call a mechanic for help. Arrive late and despondent. Reek defeat. Your interviewer will not disappoint your belief you are a loser. You will not get the job.

The second choice is Rotation. Rejoice in the good fortune the flat occurred on the driveway, not the highway. You might have been killed trying to repair it. How lucky it was a flat tire, not a blow-out at 65 miles an hour. Immediately telephone to alert your interviewer you'll be slightly late because of a tire mishap. Quickly replace the tire. Arrive at the interview exhilarated, with a ready-made conversation opener, demonstrating you are competent in practical emergencies as well as clever in your specialty. Your follow-up thank-you note will refer to your interviewer's graciousness in welcoming you slightly late, and also to your belief that awkward beginnings introduce splendid conclusions: such as your hope and expectation of obtaining the position.

Still, you may not get the job. But at very least, you will be memorable in the interviewer's long day of talking to dull, punctual, assiduous academics. Often such a trivial differentiator calls notice to real talents. Often the favorable decision between two equal contenders goes to the one who demonstrates competence under special stress. So your

chances of success may be as good or better than if you had had no flat.

More important, having rotated a road adversity into a social opportunity, you will have made a virtue of necessity. You will have avoided seeing yourself as the victim of bad luck. "Who," Lady Justine would ask, "promised you success in that job? Who promised you always perfect automobile tires?" Actually, your tire tested your ability to turn circumstance to your possible triumph. At a moment of trial you had a chance to act. Other people simply would have been acted upon. You could not unmake bad circumstance. But you could control your response to trouble. Lady Macbeth is correct when she says: "What is done cannot be undone." To this Lady Justine answers: "What is terrible can be rotated to excellence."

"Terrible," you say, "awful, soft-minded, fatalistic optimism!" You fear a treacly song about clouds' silver lining

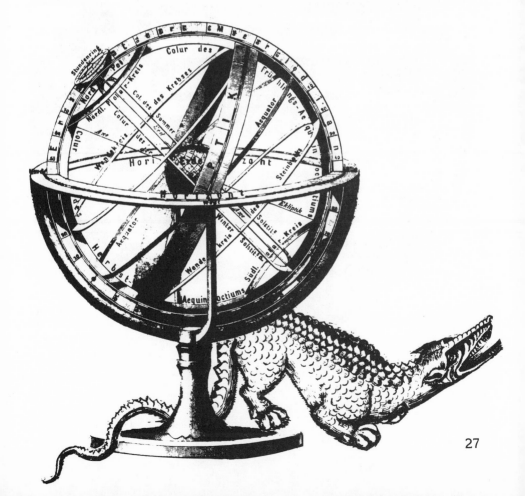

and rainstorms followed by rainbows.

"Certainly not," answers Lady Justine. "You have two choices for interpreting data: acceptance of an apparent negative, or rotation to a useful positive. Most of the world accepts the apparent negative. A few courageously rotate circumstance to personal advantage."

Consider the quick familiar test in which neutral objects, having no inherent positive or negative value, are interpreted as good or bad.

The brilliant sun on the horizon line is exactly a half orb.
Is the sun rising or setting?

The wine chalice is filled precisely halfway.
Is it half full or half empty?

The bread loaf is cut precisely in half.
Is it a despicable fragment or a welcome half loaf?

One can tilt interpretation of the neutral to either positive or negative. Far more dramatically, one can rotate adversity. Here is an example.

Yesterday your always healthy best friend was discovered to have a virulently unpleasant form of cancer. Prognosis is poor for anything beyond three years, if that. You have only two choices. First: raise your hands to heaven demanding of God why the young and the beautiful and the talented must die. Stop your work in horror and amazement at the unfair blow dealt without warning. Head in hands, repeat the word CANCER like the tolling of a death bell. You and your best friend, stunned into lamentation, helpless and hopeless, die emotionally before the actual death date. You waste whatever time is left.

Rotation is your second choice. Without malice, Lady Justine would ask you, "Who promised you long life? Who promised you good health? Or perpetual companionship?" Truly you are fortunate not to have met sudden death in the night. You will still share about three years together. How lucky that radiotherapy and chemotherapy, though nasty, will permit at least life's endurance, maybe remission, and conceivably cure. Remarkably, you change your attitude toward your job. Your perspective now is for life, for each precious day, not mere employment. You stop delaying. You decide. You take a chance on work such that in three years you and your best friend will say, "Nothing was wasted." If not for cancer's horrors and terrors you

would not have forced yourself to this renewal of purpose.

Rotation is unnervingly tough. "And," you shout, "it's irrelevant!" "Not so," says Lady Justine. "You, dear Doctor, have only two choices. One is to retrain. Go to medical school. Get a law degree. Register for the Harvard Master's degree in Business Administration. Any of these will guarantee you a better annual wage than your current Ph.D."

The only alternative to retraining is Rotation. Turn your Ph.D. adversity into opportunity. Make a virtue of necessity. Ingeniously package your academic and personal predilections. Paint your professional portrait.

You still protest that Rotation is intellectually suspect. You worry about the philosophical and political implications of this being the best of all possible worlds. You know what happened to Voltaire's Candide and Dr. Pangloss who viewed the world through rose-tinted lenses inscribed "All is for the best." This is too sweet and too pat an acceptance of evil.

Worse, Rotation allows you no chance to complain. No one commiserates. Imperious Lady Justine wants only one person to bear the responsibility and the work and the risk: You.

You really wish to get out of this. Outside it is more comfortable with those academics who moan and groan, smugly abandoning hope. They graciously offer you the cloak of delay, not revealing it is a professional death shroud. You get up to open the door to leave. Suddenly you hear a low grumbling growl of disapproval from Lady Justine's *manticore.* This monster with human head, shark's teeth, lion's body, and porcupine quills on its scorpion's tail drives you back to reality. You finally decide to acquire the five garments to clothe your naked Ph.D. figure.

Unless you are willing to risk destruction by dragon or by manticore, please go on to the first set of questions whose answers will fabricate your

Cape of Competence.

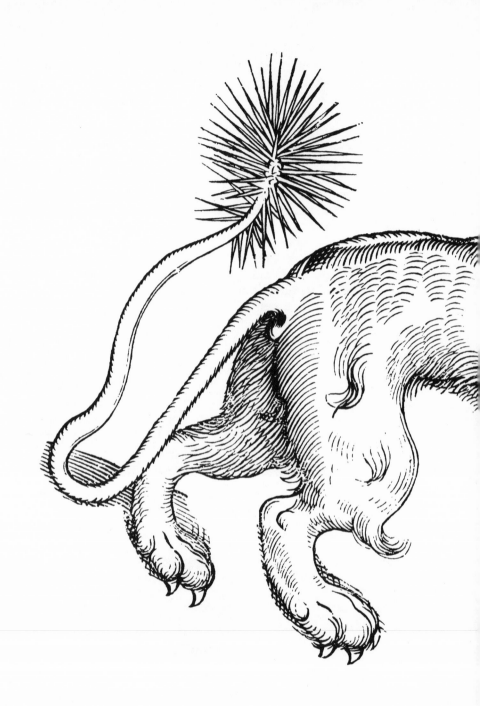

IV

Cape of
Competence

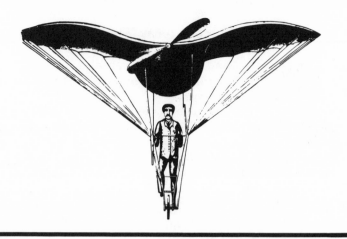

Y ou have a Ph.D. in a serious subject. Of course you are an expert. For the moment, however, that is beside the point. Excluding your specialty, what are you truly great at? What talent have you tested by experience? Lady Justine would ask you, "What, my dear, can you truly *do*?" If you say you can fly a plane, you had better be expert at handling a single engine, high-winged Cessna 172 alone at 6,000 feet. She will insist that you do. If you cannot fly, do not try. Whatever you do well, together we will honor.

However, competence does not have to be professional. You may design and sew clothes magnificently though you never have sold a garment. Also, do not worry about sex linkages. If you are truly great at plumbing or at needlework, no matter how incongruous it seems, truthfully assert your competence.

While you are at it, list what you have a true lack of ability for, namely something you have tried but know for sure you cannot do, such as navigating, for you have absolutely no sense of direction and cannot use a compass. Knowing true incompetencies sometimes is as useful as knowing genuine capabilities.

A caveat before you take offense at apparently impertinent questions. Remember, together we will discover your practical, "marketable" skills; then we will identify the market to sell them in; then "ingeniously package" marketable skills with your Ph.D. training (or some parts of it); and then sell that luminous package to a market or, if necessary, create the market.

Think, for example, of the least likely Ph.D. subject to

succeed today. The most esoteric impractical specialty money can buy perhaps is your own, or, better, Medieval and Renaissance studies.

Imagine a group of Ph.D.s whose learned dissertations concerned:

Twelfth Century Spanish Kingship Treatises

Grammar and Syntax in Medieval Latin Wandering Poets

Dance Manuals of Italian Renaissance Jewish Dance Masters

Chaucer's Poetic Music References

Portraiture of Death on Medieval Tombs and Sarcophagi.

Now think back to recent *New York Times* articles and prime time television coverage of flamboyant, historically perfect, aesthetically exciting medieval feasts and festivals presented at the Metropolitan Museum of Art, the Cloisters, the Cathedral of St. John the Divine, and elsewhere throughout the country. Perhaps you noticed the Bloomingdale's Christmas catalog of 1978 and 1979 offering tours (at $350 per person) of *Marvelous Medieval Manhattan*. Maybe you watch the popular public television show called *Medieval Splendor* or *Medieval Daily Life*. Conceivably you have read about the new geriatric advance: college courses in nursing homes which reduce elderly patients' dependence on drugs and renew their will to live. You may also have noticed surprising advertisements for data processors with medieval monks and nuns with their manuscripts competing with high technology copiers. Perhaps some relative of yours came back from Bamberger's or from such a New York private school as Brearley or Dalton or New Lincoln or Chapin reporting on fantastic medieval and Renaissance performances with lecturers, dancers, jugglers, mimes, magicians, and madrigalists.

All of these and more were presented by *Historic Spectaculars: The Complete Educational Entertainment Service.* That is a group of heretofore unemployed Ph.D.s who rotated careers out of the anguish of academe. Some members earn part-time salaries sufficient for sustenance. Full-time recompense ranges between $20,000 and $120,000 per year.

Please, then, recognize that though you may never have considered combining bricklaying talent with historical linguistics, together we may.

Cape of Competence

Remember: you are to list talents tested by experience. Check off only those elements appropriate to your own abilities.

____ Swimming	____ Carpentry
____ Rowing	____ House Painting
____ Golf	____ Roofing
____ Tennis	____ Electrical Wiring
____ Basketball	____ Ordering Closets
____ Baseball	____ Designing Spaces
____ Bicycling	____ Arranging Furniture
____ Cross-country Skiing	____ Typing
____ Snorkeling	____ Filing
____ Flying Airplanes	____ Library Research
____ Navigating	____ Archival Retrieval
____ Traffic Control	____ Exterminating
____ Stamp Collecting	____ Demolition
____ Coin Collecting	____ Sound Effects
____ Embroidery	____ Scuba Diving
____ Sewing	____ Chess
____ Critiquing. Television	____ Billiards
____ Music Criticism	____ Poker
____ Costume Design	____ Gambling
____ Shoe Making	
____ Hat Design	
____ Goldsmithery	
____ Woodworking	
____ Listening to Music	
____ Jewelry Making	
____ Stone Faceting	
____ Polishing Silver	
____ Truck Driving	
____ Taxi Driving	
____ Masonry	
____ Bricklaying	
____ Plumbing	

_____ Story-telling
_____ Bartending
_____ Drinking
_____ Waiting on Tables
_____ Sculpture
_____ Oil Painting
_____ Budget Making
_____ Spending Money
_____ Popularizing Ideas
_____ Archaeological Digging
_____ Translating
_____ Languages
_____ American Sign Language
_____ Braille
_____ Ham Radio
_____ Training Animals
_____ Grooming Animals

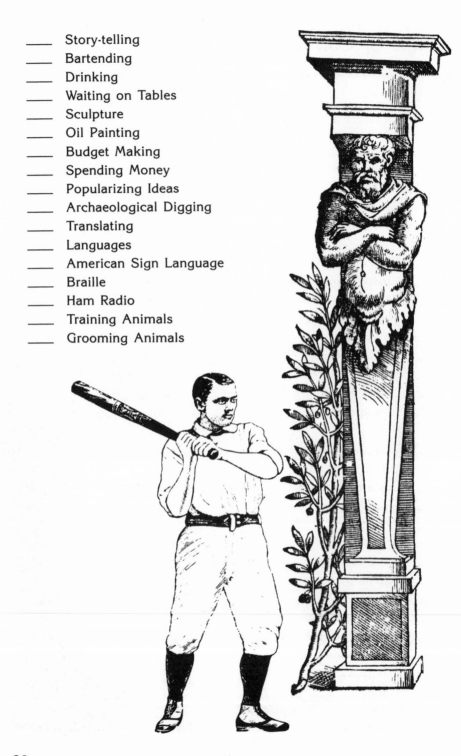

- ____ Being a Nudnick
- ____ Grave Rubbing
- ____ Auto Repair
- ____ Computer Programming
- ____ Computer Repair
- ____ Computer Graphics
- ____ Computer Design
- ____ Layout and Paste-Up
- ____ Three-Dimensional Models
- ____ Weight Lifting
- ____ Telephone Argument
- ____ Self-Defense
- ____ Store Window Display
- ____ Shopping
- ____ Housecleaning
- ____ Party Giving
- ____ Hosting and Greeting
- ____ Poster Making
- ____ Calligraphy
- ____ Printing
- ____ Inspiring
- ____ Leading
- ____ Following
- ____ Complaining
- ____ Disc Jockeying
- ____ Cooking
- ____ Baking
- ____ Wine Tasting
- ____ Making Love
- ____ Playing Wind Instruments
- ____ Playing String Instruments
- ____ Playing Keyboard Instruments
- ____ Singing
- ____ Dancing
- ____ Miming

- ____ Magic
- ____ Acting
- ____ Scenic Design
- ____ Lighting
- ____ Balancing Impossible Loads
- ____ _____
- ____ _____
- ____ _____

V

Gown of Compatibility

For this set of questions you must think of two types of talents. First consider a talent alone, then with a second ability simultaneously, while matching both of them with a third. My question is: "Could you do *it* with X?" Here the first *it* is the subject of your Ph.D.: classical languages, mechanical engineering, clinical psychology, medieval history, whatever. The second *it* must refer to one or more of the competencies you honestly revealed in the last question set. Think seriously about each question not in terms of the usual but the possible.

For example, while very few programs are dedicated to transmitting mechanical engineering to the blind, could you do it? Could your engineering degree, ability in Braille, facility in three-dimensional plastic model making, pleasure in verbal rather than visual explanation, allow you to do *it* with the blind? Several well-endowed projects for transmitting technological subjects to the handicapped need capable personnel.

Also consider these unlikely successes. A medieval literature specialist from Harvard, who never would have thought of entering the cultural boondocks, adores flying, contemplating experimental aircraft, and warm weather. He is now humanities professor at Embry-Riddle University, Florida, the Harvard of aeronautical colleges, which grants undergraduate and graduate degrees to pilots and airline business managers. He also runs their European cultural tours for students in a fine old DC 3, happily site-hopping. Another: a Ph.D. in American history, experienced with recording for the blind and computer-assisted reading machines, is theater director for the Lighthouse for the Blind; he produces in-house theater as therapy for blind students as well as public performances joining professional sighted and sightless actors in historically accurate, classic repertoire. He writes articles on American legislation relating to the handicapped and on American utopias for them.

As, no doubt, you surmise, we will look for your compatibilities with three general categories of institutions:
1. "Unlikely" colleges and universities
2. Educational programs in cultural institutions
3. Enterprising projects in businesses.

Remember also the four cases of brilliant Ph.D.s in Chapter II, *Fashions for Philosophy Doctors.*

Gown of Compatibility

____ Gifted Children

____ Retarded Children

____ Animals

____ Elderly

____ Medical Centers

____ Physicians

____ Physiotherapists

____ Asthmatics

____ Cancer Patients

____ Arthritics

____ Spelunkers

____ Librarians

____ Ships

____ Trains

____ Airplanes

____ Cars

____ Veterinarians

____ Zoologists

____ Theater Directors

____ Retailers

____ Stores

____ Department Stores

____ Electronics Manufacturers

____ Polluted Cities

____ Solar Installations

____ Graveyards

____ Terminally Ill People

____ Scuba Equipment

____ Toys

____ Gadgets

____ Farmers

____ Foresters

____ Executives	____ Stutterers
____ Preservationists	____ Handicapped People
____ Books	____ Blind People
____ Historic Houses	____ Addicts
____ Ruins	____ Dispossessed People
____ Rich People	____ Bored People
____ Poverty-line People	____ Suburban Matrons
____ Welfare Mothers	____ Unemployed People
____ Foreigners in America	____ Machines
____ Foreigners Abroad	____ Jewels
____ Unions	____ Veterans
____ Alcoholics	____ Garbage Collectors

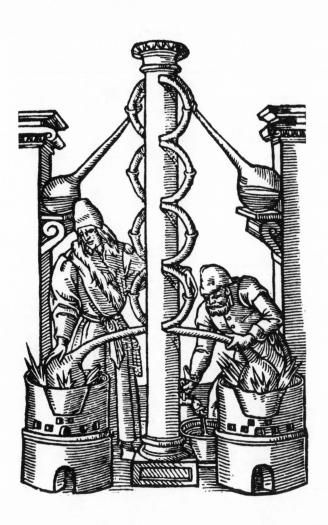

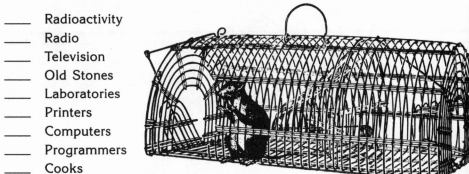

_____

_____

VI

Boots of Restriction and Spurs of Incentive

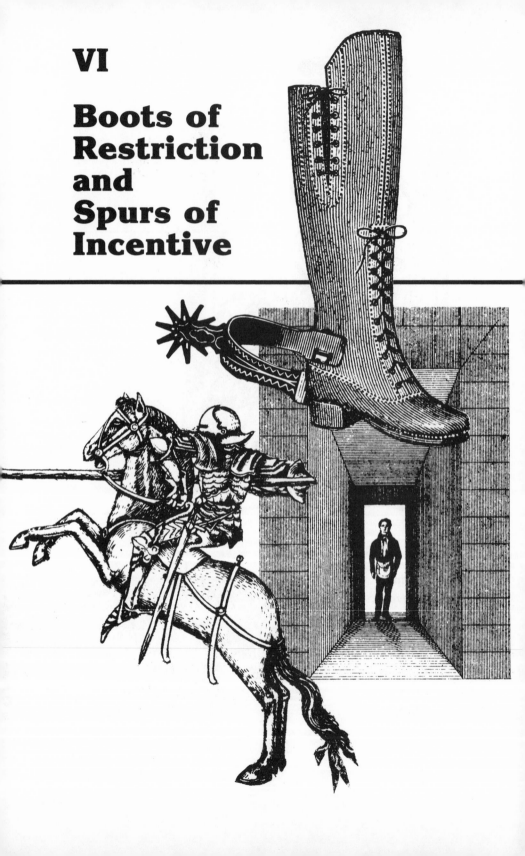

Consider a set of personal cataclysms. Some powerful event or dramatic circumstance keeps you bound to a person or place, or spurs you to escape. Recognize it, examine it honestly, then rotate it to your advantage. Be excruciatingly truthful.

Warning: this is a painful exercise. If you perform this task seriously and well, you may find yourself moved or agitated or distressed. Wonderful. Inquiry into the personal past rarely reveals golden perfection.

A second warning: time and place are significant for success with this enterprise. Ideally, allow an hour (perhaps return to this another day after having done it once) and a quiet atmosphere free from interruption and people.

Slowly read the following list. Mostly disasters and calamities, some items are lucky escapes from trouble and a few are inspirational emotional upheavals. Perform these four steps. Step One: let each entry stimulate your recall of a true event in your own past. Each of us has experienced some situation more or less shocking which has had a lifelong effect. Write down the "title" of the cataclysm, as the list does, using a short explanatory phrase.

Step Two: Ask yourself the question: "What did this teach me?" Analyze your reaction to your adversity; freely consider effects, no matter how outlandish.

Step Three: State what your cataclysm taught you in the form of a negative rule: "I will never..."

Step Four: Now state that as a positive rule: "I will always..."

Suppose, for example, you remember painfully that a

strict parent often punished unruly behavior by locking the
recalcitrant child—you—in a dark closet. For Step One ask,
"What did it teach me?" Your answer is: "Compassion for
the battered child." Fine. You will be surprised, however,
to find the emphases change when you state what you learned as negative and positive precepts. Try Step Three, the
negative rule for your life, namely "I will never willingly
stay out after dark." The same cruel memory has an
astonishing positive impetus, as your answer reveals in Step

Four: "I will always love children's theater and lots of
money."

Complex psychological justifications are not important.
Do not be surprised if your answers seem somewhat odd.
If they are not, work harder and spend more time contemplating the question and two precepts. The aim, of
course, is not instant psychoanalysis. Rather, by creative
utilization of the effects of your past, together we will for-
mulate your ideal workplace. A Brilliant Ph.D. in Nutrition

and Physiology remembered what he had forgotten from his childhood: his six older siblings and strict parents did not appreciate his puckish pranks; they forced him to spend many hours incarcerated in the dark. After he revealed the answers ascribed above to you, we initiated the process which led to his becoming the Director of Theater Feasts for Children, an Actors Equity legitimate theater-restaurant dedicated to a child audience in a wealthy midwestern suburb. Lavishly supported by the Junior League and the local toy manufacturer, his theater plays only matinees, on weekends for families, weekdays for school groups. Morning preparations and afternoon performances neatly cover his requirement to be safe with his phobia at home by nightfall.

Boots of Restriction and Spurs of Incentive

What cataclysmic event affected your life ever after?

Your best friend's suicide
Hearing Stravinsky's *The Rite of Spring*
Caring for your cousin who died of bone cancer
The murder of the President
Your home being robbed of all mementos of your past
Performing cardiopulmonary resuscitation on a man at the theater
Discovering that the one across the table from you at the formal dinner, to whom you condemned the coddling of the handicapped, was paralyzed from the waist down
Feasting on delectable steak in Africa only to discover the meat was from your favorite zebra you had studied for the past months
Being locked in a closet as a disobedient child

Forgetting to set the alarm and missing the critical appointment.
Reading *Ivanhoe*
Being told you had a brain tumor, but the diagnosis was false
Your own child's betrayal of trust
Being attacked by the dissidents in your office
Seeing the *King Tut* exhibition in London
Surviving the Holocaust
Your loss of the six hundred dollar auction bid by a mere one hundred
 on an object later valued at four million
Your friend's joining a Hare Krishna cult
Your every letter, call, and personal approach being ignored
Your car stolen with four years' worth of research notes in the trunk
Meeting a truly honest man
Loving an unattainable one
Converting to Judaism
Your best friend's alcoholism
Having a flat tire which prevented your catching the plane that later
 crashed in Washington
Purchasing a wedding ring
Your parent's illness
The electricity failure during your concert at Carnegie Hall
Being Born Again
Seeing your former lover happily married
Your best friend's revelation that he or she is gay
Being raped

Falling in love with one of another race or religion
Your divorce
Being overweight
Stopping smoking
Surviving a car crash in which a friend died
Fighting in a foreign country
Failing a test you were certain you passed
Being told you were too talented or too good for the profession.

VII

Spectacles of
Suitability

What settings do you truly love? Never mind, for the moment, your professional interests. Do you really love ocean liners? 12,000 foot mountains? Lady Justine is not concerned about your dreams but your true passions based upon experience. Be ruthlessly truthful. Do you really prefer roadside diners to fine French restaurants? Do you have a physical aversion to cold (such as the circulatory problem called Reynaud's Syndrome) but believe the Northeast weather stimulates the intellect? Do you truly lust after the Metropolitan Museum of Art *weekly*? Or could you contain yourself with an intellectual orgy there twice a year?

Spectacles of Suitability

What do you love?

_____ Solitude
_____ Bright Lights
_____ Friendships
_____ Town Comforts
_____ City Individualism
_____ City Isolation
_____ Town Camaraderie
_____ Forests
_____ Mountains
_____ Seashore
_____ Roadside Diners
_____ Fine French Restaurants
_____ Food Shops
_____ Gambling Casinos
_____ Big Hotels
_____ Fine Country Inns
_____ Camping Grounds
_____ Hostels

___ Summer Camps	___ Nursing Homes
___ Deserts	___ Limousines
___ Beaches	___ Attics
___ Large Lakes	___ Old Clothes Shops
___ Ski Resorts	___ Circuses
___ Clothing Stores	___ Chocolate Factories
___ Fur Salons	___ Laboratories
___ Jewelry Shops	___ Theaters
___ Aquariums	___ Movie Houses
___ Zoos	___ Historic Houses
___ Lions	___ Creature Comforts
___ Lap Dogs	___ Roughing it
___ Deep Forest	___ Open Fields
___ Predictability	___ Flights of Geese
___ Nature Sanctuaries	___ Redwood Forests
___ National Parks	___ Mountain Valleys
___ Amusement Parks	___ Stable Neighborhoods
___ Geodesic Domes	___ Peripatetic Movement

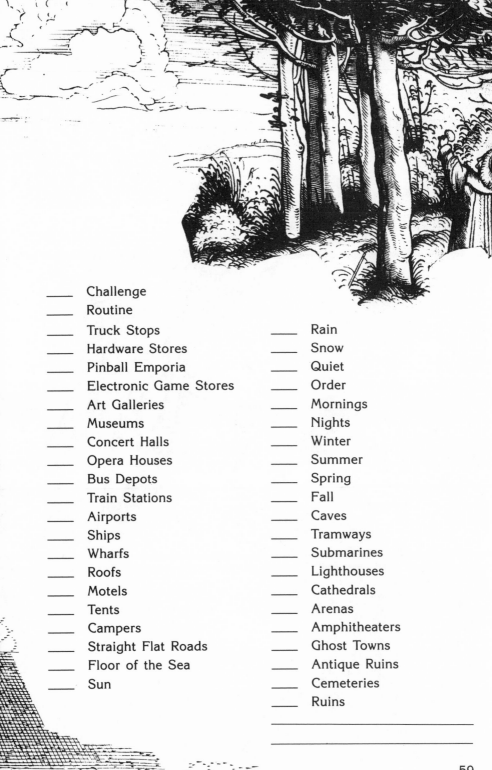

_____ Challenge
_____ Routine
_____ Truck Stops
_____ Hardware Stores
_____ Pinball Emporia
_____ Electronic Game Stores
_____ Art Galleries
_____ Museums
_____ Concert Halls
_____ Opera Houses
_____ Bus Depots
_____ Train Stations
_____ Airports
_____ Ships
_____ Wharfs
_____ Roofs
_____ Motels
_____ Tents
_____ Campers
_____ Straight Flat Roads
_____ Floor of the Sea
_____ Sun

_____ Rain
_____ Snow
_____ Quiet
_____ Order
_____ Mornings
_____ Nights
_____ Winter
_____ Summer
_____ Spring
_____ Fall
_____ Caves
_____ Tramways
_____ Submarines
_____ Lighthouses
_____ Cathedrals
_____ Arenas
_____ Amphitheaters
_____ Ghost Towns
_____ Antique Ruins
_____ Cemeteries
_____ Ruins

_____
_____

VIII
Cap of Abstraction

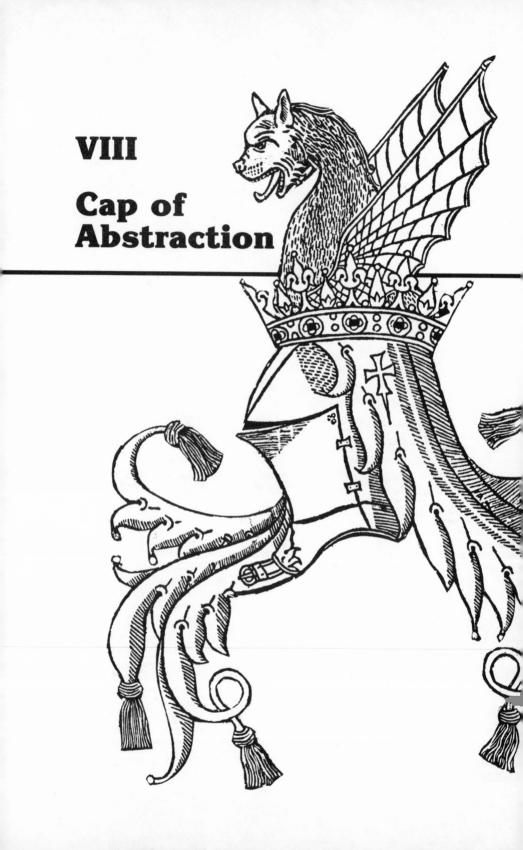

What are your true aversions and attractions? Bureaucratic delay, for example, is philosophically acceptable to some personalities but in others it dangerously raises the ire and blood pressure. If you cannot thrive on time pressure, a job with monthly publication deadlines might be unhealthy for you professionally and physically. If you know you hate deadlines, rigid routines, simple yes-no answers, slovenly work space, running, Southern drawls, or women, admit it. While you might wish to be less prejudiced, more liberal, more athletic, or less misogynous, recognize that you are what you are. Rotate your aversions to your advantage. Similarly celebrate, honestly, the ideas you love.

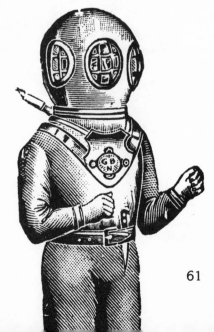

Cap of Abstraction

Rank each abstract or concrete idea by a number from 1 through 4.
1 = with anger
2 = with avoidance
3 = with acceptance
4 = with pleasure
Each entry ought to have only one number, of course.

How do you respond to:

_____ Mediocrity
_____ Ambiguity
_____ Folly
_____ Fools
_____ Inefficiency
_____ Unfairness
_____ Perfidy
_____ Arrogance
_____ Stupidity
_____ Bureaucracy
_____ Red Tape
_____ Rigid Routines
_____ Delay
_____ Chaos
_____ Hurry
_____ Rushing
_____ Deadlines
_____ Physical Disability
_____ Ruthlessness
_____ Condescension
_____ Pity
_____ Women
_____ Homosexuals
_____ Jews
_____ Short People
_____ Fat People

_____ Lady Bosses
_____ Sexual Advances
_____ Circumlocution
_____ Jargon
_____ Dirt
_____ Odor of Urine
_____ Yes-No Answers
_____ Multiple Choices
_____ Rhetoric
_____ Slovenliness
_____ Impeccable Order
_____ Condescension to Children
_____ Running
_____ Sitting
_____ Smooth Talk
_____ Vague Speech
_____ New Ideas
_____ Stress
_____ Creationism
_____ Liberalism
_____ Blackmail
_____ Serendipity
_____ Surprises
_____ Wealth
_____ Poverty
_____ Money Grubbing

____ Comfort	____ Change
____ Fear	____ Illness
____ Risks	____ Command
____ Waste	____ Total Responsibility
____ Appreciation	____ Development
____ Compliments	____ Foreigners
____ Pomposity	____ Garbage
____ Ignoring	____ Obsequiousness
____ Failure	____ Contempt
____ Triumph	____ Lying
____ Fame	____ Darwinism
____ Testing	____ Southern Drawls
____ Leisure	____ Excessive Noise
____ Retirement	____ Slow Motion
____ Old People	____ Lady Justine
____ Insolence	_____
____ Schnorers	_____
____ Preservation	_____

IX
The Dragon

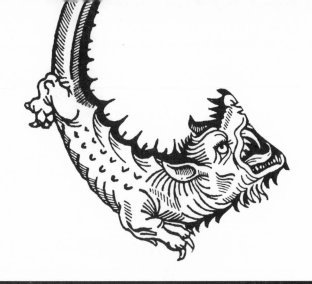

Now real work begins. You must practice a creative double nature. You are both the analyst of data and the stuff studied. You are scholar and subject. With a clear distinction between what you truly see and what you wish you had seen, bravely begin the tasks of Correlating, Templating, Researching, and Proposing. These simply are variations upon what you were trained to do in your doctoral specialty. All four jobs are tough. Naturally. If you could exert yourself in the past for your subject, department, or professors, certainly you can succeed as well for yourself. Before beginning, however, you had better cultivate a necessary though unfashionable talent: Kissing the Dragon.

Lady Justine tells this story called "The Sovereignty of Erin."

Once upon a very long time ago an old man named Nyall lived at the edge of a grand dark forest with his nine sons. One night Nyall called his sons to him and said, "My men, our forest and our fields are being destroyed by fire. Soon even we ourselves shall be burned up. A fierce, foul, ferocious, fire-fuming dragon is consuming everything living in its way. We must kill it, or surely it will kill us."

The first and oldest son of Nyall said, "Father, let me go deep into the forest to the dragon's lair. I have strong armor and a sharp sword. I have fought fierce dragons before. I will rid this place of that terror."

So the first son of Nyall walked proudly through the trees. He heard the creaking and rattling of the dragon's wings. He felt the heat of the flames flaring from its nostrils. He

saw the dragon's loathsome scaly head. He crept closer and closer. He saw the terrible armored claws. Slowly the dragon was aware of him. Suddenly it wheeled round and shrieked with a loud piercing wail, "Kiss me!"

Astonished and dismayed, the first son of Nyall ran from the forest. Fear and revulsion kept him from ever looking back.

The second night the second son of Nyall said, "Father, let me go into the forest to kill the dragon. I have strong arms and have long studied warfare against dragons. I will kill this terrible beast." So the second son walked carefully, approaching the dragon from behind. He heard the creaking scales, saw the powerful wings, and strong fierce jaws. He shouted as he lunged with his sword. No metal could pierce that beastly body. The dragon shook with a horrible roar, shouting, "Kiss me!" The terrified young knight fled from the forest.

On the third night the third son ventured, and the fourth night the fourth son, and so each in succession tried to kill the dragon. But the forest was getting smaller and the fires brighter as each night passed. At last, only the ninth son was left. Old Nyall said, "Oh my son, you cannot go alone into the dragon fight where all your brothers have failed. You are my youngest. You have no experience with dragons. You do not even have proper fighting armor."

"Father," said the youngest son, "I must go. I have studied dragons. I will rid this forest of that beastly menace."

So the ninth and youngest son of Nyall entered the forest armed only with his small sword. He walked quietly and carefully towards the dragon. When the dragon shrieked "Kiss me!" the young man summoned all his courage, pursed his lips, and pressed them, kissing, on the dragon's stinking neck. Suddenly the fierce, foul, ferocious, fire-fuming dragon vanished. In its place was an exquisitely beautiful princess. "Thank you for releasing me from enchantment. I am The Sovereignty of Erin. Come live with me and be my love. Together we will rule the kingdom." And so they did, merrily ever after.

This fiery dragon clearly is more than what she seems. Who and what is this shape-shifter? Sovereignty means, of course, kingship or rulerdom. Erin or Ireland is the country controlled. The dragon is kingship itself which the youngest son merited. His virtue was defined by trial. Others boasted and failed. He acted properly and prevailed. Apparently the least likely of the nine brothers, he truly was

the most ingenious, most adventurous, and most thoroughly courageous. He dared to risk himself, unarmed, to do what was requested and required. It worked. His eight brothers, well prepared at knight school, could not adapt lessons of warfare to requirements for love.

The truly strong know that restraint of great prowess is harder than display of power. Just as martial aggressiveness often hides inherent weakness, so gentleness often displays inherent might. True power balances, in time, freedom with control, plan with intuitive boldness.

Moreover, though leadership commonly is thought to be rich pomp and splendor, it is despicably difficult, responsible work. To be vested with enormous authority is an extreme form of servitude. Only the one prepared for the draconic perils of office merits its princely pleasures.

"Please," Lady Justine interrupts, "get to the painful point." Powerful steely-armed warriors, disarmed by the necessity for courageous tenderness, demonstrate that life does not necessarily provide the chance to practice what one has trained for. To put it another way, while one carefully trains for meeting one world, that world may change. Or, intelligent people deceive themselves into believing a changed world has not changed. Or, no matter how hard or well or magnificently one practices special skills, not only they but the total self will be tested in the hour of crisis.

Training is wonderful but arbitrary. The specialty is only the superficial faceting and polishing of the inherent intellectual radiance. That brilliance is what Erin required of its king, and life requires of its most intelligent beings. The whole intelligence is on trial, not merely the exercises of its parts. Any medical professor knows that students who excel at basic theoretical science and anatomy often prove absolute ninnies when applying theory to the real patient. Knowing all the answers for the abstract disease, the student cannot see the patient's symptoms which deviate from the textbook description. The medical student expecting to see "elephant" is nonplussed when confronting "crow." Seeing the beak and hearing the caw he still keeps looking for the trunk and tail and so diagnoses black crow as "stunted melanotic elephant."

Just as theories and facts must be integrated creatively with common sense, so Ph.D. training alone is not the essential being but only the naked stick figure garbed in a gold-tasseled mortarboard. Therefore Lady Justine insists you

clothe yourself in the *Cape of Competence, Gown of Compatibility, Boots of Restriction* with their *Spurs of Incentive, Spectacles of Suitability,* and *Cap of Abstraction.*

Of course you perceive the inevitable nastiest moral of "The Sovereignty of Erin." To be king one must kiss the dragon. To escape destruction by the Dragon of Discontent (or Academic Dissatisfaction or Underemployment or Starvation), one must boldly transform it.

"Kissing a dragon," you say, "is disgusting, revolting, and terrifying." True. And there is always the danger that the dragon might not shift shape but simply gobble down the kisser, lips to toes. But Lady Justine reminds you about Rotation and her wheel. If your forest is being consumed and there is no one left to save it, then you are lucky to have the chance to salvage your trees and your life. You are fortunate you will know the exhilaration of the struggle, and, we hope, the glory of triumph. It is good that you have so fine an adversary in that radiantly fierce, foul, ferocious, fire-fuming dragon. Anything less would not be worth your pain. No gift given ever will equal that battle fought and won.

Rotating your adversity into opportunity—or Kissing the Dragon—requires your assertive, attentive, ethical commitment to one of the most significant beings in the world: yourself. To the exclusion of other duties, you must now practice a Benign Selfishness. You must ask yourself what the great Hebrew sage Hillel counseled:

If not I, who?

If not now, when?

Answer "I!" and "Now!" Begin the chores of *Dragon Kissing.*

X

Correlating or Dragon Kissing I

On five sheets of paper, each titled for one of your Five Fashionable Garments for Philosophy Doctors, transcribe your answers from the question sets. If you answered these questions scrupulously, fairly, and honestly, you will be somewhat surprised at your own judgments of your competences and capabilities. For each answer to each question, you must now ask two more questions. Then you must make scholarly sense of the answers. These are the apparently simple but inherently difficult questions:

    1.   What are the essentials?

    2.   What are the implications?

For the *Cape of Competence,* for example, suppose you included *rowing* for a college crew team. You must ask: What are the essentials? What are the implications? As with any true definition, there are literal "dictionary meanings" of the word. Denotations of rowing are specific, predictable, and fixed. Rowing is maneuvering an oar while seated in a long slender lightweight boat in order to propel it on the water, usually in a race, as a member of a team of two, six, or eight rowers, directed by a coxswain, requiring intense physical exertion, bodily discipline, and obedience to command. Connotations of rowing include: Ability of the rower to subsume desires of self to necessity of the team. A willingness to act immediately upon orders. Capacity to reach beyond the usual bounds of physical exertion when inspired by the team. Training and working not simply to participate but to win. Enduring long months of muscle and endurance building for tests (races) of only minutes duration. Ability to persevere under adverse physical con-

ditions (heat, cold, and wet) and intense disappointment (losing).

Implications and essentials of *ordering closets* differ markedly. Of course one talent is not superior to the other. Certainly one person may possess both. However the essentials of closet ordering are: the establishment and actualization of a logical plan for assembling and making accessible many objects in a small enclosed space, the arrangements using shelves, rods, boxes and other separating devices. Implications are: ability to conceive and execute independently a practical plan for retrieving objects or information. Capacity to work without guidance or companionship for one's own or others' benefit. Interest in hierarchy and compartmentalization. Concern for categorization and collecting rather than dispensing and disposing.

"Come now," you protest. "Surely this is over-much interpretation for the simple words *rowing* and *closets.*" "Not at all," retorts Lady Justine. "While it is dangerous to read too much into answers, it is deadly to leave out important qualities. Intellectuals often discount intellectual components of the more menial and craftsmanlike activities in which they themselves are expert. Consider electrical wiring. In the Cape of Competence, a Brilliant Ph.D. in Art History listed *wiring,* having worked for many years doing practical electrical engineering for a suburban lighting fixture company. Essentials: planning, running wire, and installing ceiling and wall electrical incandescent and fluorescent fixtures for homes and small businesses. While an overalls job, not coat and tie, it had fascinating connotations. Reluctantly at first, then jubilantly, we discovered together that *electrical wiring* implied:

1. Ability to plan, then successfully utilize dangerous materials in complex hidden patterns (stringing wires from the main line or major circuit box through walls and ceilings, indoor and outdoor conduits).

2. A habit of checking the plan and its actualization multiple times at critical junctures before conclusion (testing the viability of each major "branch" from the electrical "trunk" wire).

3. Capacity to transform unpredictable personal requirements of householder or businessman into financially reasonable project, permitting adherence to the client's

budget plus profitable return on the boss's time and material.

4. An ability to satisfy often conflicting demands of customer and boss, therefore a good mediator between extremes.

5. Flair for utilizing standard mass-produced components in individualistic manner, and an ingenuity in rearrangement of existing elements for new purposes, as adaptation of industrial, track, and decorative lighting

schemes to kitchens or store window displays. Thus a talent for synthesis rather than creation.

We will apply these data to a job later, in Chapter XIII, *Proposing.*

As for your own aptitudes, ask the two questions:

1. What are the essentials?
2. What are the implications?

for each and every element you have listed for each one of the Five Garments. You may have five pages or a thick sheaf. If you were absolutely, magnificently honest, your answers will fall into a repetitive pattern. The essentials of your *Cape* resemble the essentials of your *Gown* resemble the essentials of your *Boots and Spurs* resemble the essentials of your *Spectacles* and of your *Cap.* A pattern also will emerge for the answers to the second question on implications. Correlating and pattern-making, you will have begun the job of pattern-finder, namely *Templating.*

XI
Templating or Dragon Kissing II

What the prepared eye looks for, it finds. Your quest is for that pattern of your talents and predilections which will be your work Template: a general design you will impose upon possibility. Your intention is to identify, and, if necessary, to create a job with, as Lady Justine insisted in Chapter I, salary, current reward, and future hope.

A Brilliant Ph.D. in Developmental Psychology had these five fashionable garments.

Cape: private pilot, with instrument rating, currently working for a commercial license; aeronautical history buff; capable photographer.

Gown: libraries, museums, and historical collections.

Boots and *Spurs:* enduring, at age seven, his father's death from an industrial accident; yielding *spurs,* an endearing but insatiable questioning of "why?" for every personal and social phenomenon.

Spectacles: any predictable topography, no extremes in climate, no wild waves, no eroding beaches.

Cap: hatred of sloppy language, slovenly workplace, disorder, and chaos.

What might be the reasonable Template? Remember we are looking for a pattern which will be useful in generating a job in one of three types of sites:

Class I: "Unlikely" colleges and universities
Class II: Educational sections of cultural institutions
Class III: Enterprising projects for business or industry.

The Template records ideal combinations of talents and preferences. Naturally, the world has no obligation to ar-

range itself to your Template. But if you create it cleverly you may compel surprising congruence.

The Template is like the Medieval and Renaissance *mirror*. Wonderful books of instruction and advice for princes are called *Mirrors for Princes*. Presentations of perfect legal manners appeared in *Mirrors for Magistrates*. The prince or judge looking into a *Mirror* could see the ideal and then try to reflect it in his personal life. Your work Template is the perfect job ingeniously packaging your personal talents and predilections. Reality need not conform to the ideal. But it ought to come close.

The Template for the Brilliant Ph.D. in Developmental Psychology:

A curatorial or editorial post in an aeronautical college, library, or museum, allowing investigation of the personal achievements, as opposed to their purely technological feats, of early airplane designers and aviators.

"Bizarre," you say. "Certainly not," reminds Lady Justine. "The world is wide and glorious. The prepared eye finds what it seeks." "But where," you ask, "does the unprepared eye start looking?"

That question introduces a practical talent every Ph.D. is good at: *Researching,* also known as *Dragon Kissing III.*

XII

Researching or Dragon Kissing III

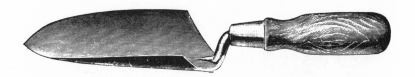

$\mathbf{A}$ good research library is familiar territory to a Ph.D. A mediocre research library will do. A city or town library also might serve, provided it has certain basic guides and indexes or, better, a competent congenial librarian.

You will spend many days researching. However, think how much library time you expended for your thesis or dissertation. That was a mere requirement for your degree. This research is prerequisite for your life's work. It will be well worth a week's excursion to a good library if one is not nearby. Consider your own or former university. This will be an investment of time, money, and spirit. But if you prorate your expenditures over the next twenty years of your successful work life, the percentage of return will be staggeringly high, a truly gilt-edged investment.

Armed with five-by-eight file cards, at least three hundred, a file-case with separators, plus pens and pencils, you will begin looking for those books likely to yield the names, addresses, phone numbers, and specific details on size, qualities, and leading personnel of organizations fitting your personal Template. Naturally, you will create a card for each and every reference book you use for your Template bibliography, for you may have to check the reference works again.

Your Template catalog will have a separate card for each of the many institutions' names for each of your three classes of data:

1. Unlikely colleges and universities
2. Educational divisions of cultural institutions
3. Enterprising projects in business or industry.

Imagine, for example, research for the Brilliant Ph.D. in Developmental Psychology. Information is required for Class 1: Unlikely Colleges. Numerous aeronautical colleges exist in various parts of the country. Their essential data are available in the many traditional guides to institutions of higher learning. Check the references not only for vital statistics but important asides, such as this: Embry-Riddle University in Daytona Beach, Florida, the "Harvard" of the aeronautical colleges, has "an extensive new" aeronautical library collection. In addition to its academic departments, its library also might require a curator or researcher or scholarly interpreter.

More information for the unlikely colleges of Class 1, as well, of course, as for Class 2 (educational projects in cultural institutions), comes from particular treasuries of specific data. For everything there is a season and a reference book. Just to begin, look at: Allan, John, L., *Aviation and Space Museums of America* (New York: Arco, 1975).

American Association of Museums, *The Official Museum Directory* (New York, National Register Publishing Co., 1982). And *Museums of the World/Museum der Welt* (Munchen: Verlag Dokumentation, 1973). Read the following excerpts from that wondrous compilation of necessary information on almost any discrete topic, Lee Ash's *Special Collections: A Guide to Special Book Collections and Subject Emphases as Reported by University, College, Public, and Special Libraries and Museums in the United States and Canada* (New York and London: R. R. Bowker Co., 1978).

Though drab in title, *Subject Collections* is an exciting idea hoard. Note that important universities such as Cal Tech, Stanford, and Claremont Colleges have significant "personal" aeronautical collections of books and memorabilia. While their academic departments might be hopeless for entering, their aeronautical collections might be accessible.

Class 2: Museums and Cultural Institutions, includes some surprises. The Smithsonian's National Air and Space Museum Bureau boasts not less than 22,000 catalogued aeronautical volumes, including maps, pictures, slides, and microforms, a huge picture collection, over 600,000 photos, and even a 1500 piece collection of aeronautical music. NASA's Ames Research Libraries at Moffett Field, California, with a listed budget of $260,000, has an aerospace medical collection which specifically includes the behavioral sciences. Note also the municipal libraries and museums in smaller towns and larger cities. And do not ignore the

privately endowed collections; one of the most scholarly, intellectually elegant, and physically opulent library-museums in the country is the Burndy Library in Norwalk, Connecticut, the work of the industrialist-inventor-philanthropist, Dr. Bern Dibner. By now you are beginning to see possibilities for employment in a host of institutions you may never have thought of for a most unlikely set of talents and predilections.

As for Class 3, not only the Air Transport Association of America might be a good employment lead, but such corporations as Northrop, McDonall Douglas , United Air Lines, Pan American World Airways, Boeing, Rockwell International's Space Division, Bendix, General Dynamics, Bell Telephone Labs, and IBM all have, to greater or lesser degree, some holdings which might serve the purpose of employing the Brilliant Ph.D.

These are the research pickings from only a few books. Of course, most of the entries on cards for all three classes of data will be non-contributory. That is the nature, after all, of most preliminary research. No scholarly or scientific research immediately turns theory into fact. And there is always the possibility of that great tragedy of scholarship

or science (as T. H. Huxley reminds us), the slaying of a
beautiful hypothesis by an ugly fact. The ideal place may
have no budget; its by-laws may prohibit it from accepting
Brilliant Ph.D.s in Developmental Psychology. No matter.
Persevere. Research is inquiry and investigation. If answers
are self-evident and easy, there would be no challenge, or
Dragon.

When the heroic research job is complete, you will have
hundreds of possibilities. Reason and discretion will require
your winnowing away the extraneous chaff to isolate the
essential kernels. You should have a minimum of seven
institutions listed for each of the three classes and a max-
imum of 33. The three categories, of course, have no requirement for equality of number or substance. Prepare
to write between 21 and 99 letters with proposals. But before
that, you must plot. This comes naturally to entrepreneurs,
Machiavellians, and students of *Dragon Kissing IV:
Proposing.*

Excerpts from Typical Entries in Ash's Special Collections

AERONAUTICS

Northrop Corporation, Aircraft Group, Library Services Dept. H. W. Jones, Manager. 3901 W. Broadway, Hawthorne, **Calif.** 90250
Vols. (15,000) Cat. Microforms
Budget ($27,000)
Notes: Incl. file of military specifications and standards, Air Force Technical Orders, and other military manuals, handbooks, regulations, instructions, etc. Also 250,000 microfiche; 60,000 reports. Library use restricted to employees; others by interlibrary loan.

†McDonnell Douglas Corp., Douglas Aircraft Company, Technical Library. Meryl H. Swanigan, Libn. 3855 Lakewood Blvd., Box 200, Long Beach, **Calif.** 90846
Vols. 12,000 Cat. Microforms

NASA, Ames Research Center, Libraries. Ralph W. Lewis, Chief, Library Br. 202–3, Moffett Field, **Calif.** 94035
Vols. (70,000) Cat. Audiotapes Microforms
Budget ($260,000)
Notes: Main library collections cover physical sciences, engineering and mathematical fields related to research programs in aeronautics–space research. Life sciences library collections cover medical, physiological, behavioral and biological sciences related to research programs. Also emphasis on remote sensing of earth resources and the search for extraterrestrial life. 700 journal titles.

†California Institute of Technology, Aeronautics Library. Pasadena, **Calif.** 91109
Vols. 9000 Cat.

United Air Lines, Engineering Dept., Library. J. J. Whitney, Technical Libn. San Francisco International Airport, San Francisco, **Calif.** 94128
Vols. 4500 Cat.
Budget ($5500)
Notes: Mostly current books on technical aspects; some history books.

†Aurora Public Library. Mary Brown, City Libn. 1298 Peoria St., Aurora, **Colo.** 80011
Vols. 1000 Cat. Maps Pix. Slides Microforms

U.S. Air Force Academy, Library. Benjaman C. Glidden, Dir. USAF Academy, **Colo.** 80840
Vols. 6400 Cat. Mss. Maps Pix. Microforms

Yale University Libraries, Manuscripts & Archives. Box 1603A, Yale Sta., New Haven, **Conn.** 06520

Air Transport Association of America, Library. Ms. Marion Mistrik, Libn. 1709 New York Ave. N.W., Washington, **D.C.** 20006
Vols. 14,000 Cat. Maps Pix. Microfilm
Budget ($6000)
Notes: Emphasis of collection is air transport, its history and economics. Incl. standard transportation texts, official administrative and statistical reports of the regulatory agencies, Congressional documents, annual reports of U.S. scheduled airlines, and a limited number of technical reports.

University of Illinois, Urbana/Champaign. Library. Len Coburn, Coordinator of Engineering Library Services. 221 Engineering Hall, Urbana, **Ill.** 61801
Vols. (158,540) Cat. Slides Microforms
Budget ($32,500)
Notes: Plus 1602 journal titles, 1740 continuation titles. Collection designed to serve teaching and research programs. Supports faculty research. Also, 470 microfilm reels and 4015 microfiche sheets.

Purdue University Libraries/AVC. Engineering Library. Edwin D. Posey, Engineering Libn. A. A. Potter Engineering Center, W. Lafayette, **Ind.** 47907
Vols. (117,301) Cat. Maps Audiotapes Microforms
Budget ($152,473)

University of Massachusetts/Amherst Libraries, Physical Sciences Library. Vlasta K. Greenbie, Head. Amherst, **Mass.** 01003
Vols. (108,000) Cat. Microforms
Notes: Incl. extensive holdings of journals, NACA and NASA publications, and AEC documents (microfiche).

†Federal Aviation Administration, Central Region Library. Norene Copeland, Libn. Federal Bldg., Rm. 1556, 601 E. 12 St., Kansas City, **Mo.** 64106.
Vols. (7000) Maps Microforms

†Princeton University Library. Vladimir Simosko, Libn. Forrestal Campus Library. Princeton, **N.J.** 08540
Vols. 21,000 Cat.

Polytechnic Institute of New York, Long Island Center Library. Lorraine Schein, Libn. Route 110, Farmingdale, **N.Y.** 11735
Vols. 2000 Cat. Microforms
Budget $1000

American Institute of Aeronautics & Astronautics, Technical Information Service. Patricia Marshall, Chief Libn. 750 Third Ave., New York. **N.Y.** 10017
Vols. (57,000) Cat. Microforms
Notes: Basis of published literature input to NASA Information System; Special index—Semimonthly issues of *International Aerospace Abstracts* with cumulated semiannual and annual indexes.

†Columbia University Libraries, Engineering Library. 535 W. 114 St., New York, **N.Y.** 10027
Vols. (90,000) Cat.
Notes: All aspects of engineering—aeronautical, industrial mining, civil, chemical, mechanical, electrical, nuclear. Incl. applied mathematics and applied physical sciences. Over (530,000) technical reports.

New York Public Library, Research Libraries. Robert G. Krupp, Chief, Science and Technology Research Center. Fifth Ave. & 42 St., New York, **N.Y.** 10018
Vols. (750,000) Cat. Microforms

Pan American World Airways, Corporate Library. Liwa Chiu, Libn. 200 Park Ave., New York, **N.Y.** 10017
Vols. 450 Uncat. 16mm Films Microforms
Budget $2500
Notes: No photocopying.

Dowling College, Library. John R. Beard, Dir. Idle Hour Blvd., Oakdale, **N.Y.** 11769
Vols. 500 Cat.
Budget $700

†Rochester Museum & Science Center, Strasenburgh Planetarium, Todd Library. Donald Hall, Dir. 663 East Ave., Rochester, **N.Y.** 14607
Vols. 500 Cat. Maps Slides
Notes: Also, 8000 slides of astronomical and aeronautical subjects; 400 recordings; 150 celestial charts.

†Yonkers Public Library. Elinor L. Upton, Technical Libn., Technical & Business Dept. 70 S. Broadway, Yonkers, **N.Y.** 10701
Vols. (19,300) Cat. Maps Microforms
Budget ($15,500)

Akron-Summit County Public Library. Joyce McKnight, Head, Science & Technology Div. 55 S. Main St.,

Akron, **Ohio** 44326
Vols. 760 Cat. Pix.
Notes: The Lighter-Than-Air Society book collection is in the Akron Public Library. Incl. foreign language books.

Ohio State University, Engineering Library. Mary Jo V. Arnold, Libn. 2024 Neil Ave., Columbus, **Ohio** 43210
Vols. (120,000) Cat. Microforms
Budget ($40,000)

Alliance College, Washington Hall Library. Stanley J. Kozacka, Head Libn. Fullerton Ave., Cambridge Springs, **Pa.** 16403
Vols. (5844) Cat.
Notes: A NASA depository of declassified documents.

Franklin Institute Library. Emerson W. Hilker, Dir. 20 & The Parkway, Philadelphia, **Pa.** 19103
Vols. (300,000) Cat. Maps Pix. Microforms
Budget ($180,000)

University of Pennsylvania, Towne Scientific Library. Rose E. Lonberger, Libn. 220 S. 33 St., Philadelphia, **Pa.** 19104
Vols. (65,000) Cat.
Budget ($57,000)

South Dakota School of Mines & Technology. Devereaux Library. Philip E. McCauley, Dir. Rapid City, **S.D.** 57701
Vols. (3000) Uncat. Maps Pix. Slides Audiotapes 16mm Films Filmstrips
Notes: A somewhat limited Aviation Resource Center to an area approx. 90,000 sq. miles in breadth and width, covering western South Dakota; western North Dakota; western Nebraska; eastern Montana; eastern Wyoming; and northeast corner of Colorado. Materials incl. are books, periodicals, posters, pictures, etc., from NASA, FAA and various aviation and aeronautics-related companies in the U.S.

Rice University, Fondren Library. Richard L. O'Keeffe, Libn. 6100 S. Main St. (Mailing add.: P.O. Box 1892), Houston, **Tex.** 77001

Boeing Company, Kent Technical Library. Ruth E. Shipp, Libn. P.O. Box 3999, Seattle, **Wash.** 98124
Vols. (25,000) Cat. Microforms
Notes: Library restricted to Boeing personnel. Kent Technical Library is the former Aerospace Division/Aerospace Group Technical Library.

Seattle Public Library. Ronald A. Dubberly, City Libn. 1000 Fourth Ave., Seattle, **Wash.** 98104
Vols. 20,000 Cat. Microforms

EAA Air Museum Foundation Research Library. Gene R. Chase, Dir. P.O. Box 229, Hales Corners, **Wis.** 53130
Vols. 1500 Cat. Maps Pix. Slides Films Microforms
Notes: Mostly periodicals, engineering reports, aircraft construction drawings, and other nonbook materials; also about 1500 books, mostly textbooks and historical works.

†National Research Council of Canada. Aeronautical/Mechanical Engineering Branch Library. Elizabeth Colyer, Libn. Montreal Rd., Ottawa, Ont. K1A 0R6 **Can.**
Vols. (566,074) Cat. Microforms

AERONAUTICS—BIOGRAPHY

Smithsonian Institution Libraries, National Air & Space Museum Bureau. Catherine D. Scott, Bureau Libn. NASM Bldg., Sixth & Independence Ave., S.W., Washington, **D.C.** 20560
Vols. (22,000) Cat. Mss. Maps Pix. Slides Microforms
Notes: History of flight and aerospace development, incl. biographical material on aviation pioneers, balloons and ballooning. Extensive photographic collection (600,000 pictures). Incl. the Sherman Fairchild Collection of aeronautical photographs (transferred from the American Institute of Aeronautics and Astronautics). Also incl. the Bella Landauer Aeronautical Sheet Music Collection (1500 pieces). 2000 films; 800,000 microforms; 4100 periodicals.

AERONAUTICS—HISTORY

Claremont Colleges. Norman F. Sprague Memorial Library. David Kuhner, Libn. 12 & Dartmouth, Claremont, **Calif.** 91711
Vols. 3500 Cat. Mss. Maps Pix. Phonorecords
Notes: Gift of Rev. and Mrs. John F. B. Carruthers of Pasadena, 1950. Emphasis on history of ballooning, early aviation, World War I and World War II military aviation, pioneer flyers and flights, women in aviation, cartoons, songs, memorabilia, some diaries and journals. Restricted use. Collection transferred here from Honnold Library.

Occidental College, Library. Michael C. Sutherland. Special Collections Libn. 1600 Campus Rd., Los Angeles, **Calif.** 90041
Vols. 1200 // Cat. Pix.
Notes: Northrup–Millar Aviation Collection: history of aviation and aviation industry to the 1950s.

University of California, Los Angeles. Research Library. Dept. of Special Collections. James V. Mink, Head. 405 Hilgard Ave., Los Angeles, **Calif.** 90024
Cat. Mss. Maps Pix.
Notes: Incl. the papers of Elizabeth Hiatt Gregory; 1872–1955, pioneer aviation journalist and lecturer, and Alexander Klemin, 1888–1950, aeronautical engineer and teacher. To be used under direct supervision of librarian at all times.

California Institute of Technology, Archives. Judith R. Goodstein, Archivist. 1201 E. California Blvd., Pasadena, **Calif.** 91125
Vols. (3000) Uncat. Mss. Maps Pix. Slides Phonorecords Audiotapes Videotapes 16mm Films Microforms
Notes: Over 60 collections (1830s–present) relating to history of 19th–20th centuries science and technology and the history of the Institute. Included are personal and professional papers of Caltech scientists and administrative officers; divisional records and faculty committees; over 5000 photographs of American and European scientists. Mss. collections document more than a century of American political, social, and intellectual history; the development of the physical sciences, aeronautics, molecular biology, and seismology in the U.S. and abroad; and social and political conditions in Europe between the two World Wars. There are also family letters relating to 19th century American life before and during the Civil War (the Morley papers); to 19th century social conditions in Russia and Hungary (the Paul Epstein papers and Theodore von Kármán papers); and to the development of 20th century Italian mathematics.

San Diego Aero-Space Museum, Prudden Historical Library & Archives. B. C. Reynolds, Archivist. 1649 El Prado, Balboa Park, San Diego, **Calif.** 92101
// Uncat. Microforms
Notes: 98 percent of this aeronautics and aerospace collection was destroyed by fire in early 1978. The only item saved was a large scrapbook of newspaper clippings (1913–14) compiled by Hillery Beachey.

†San Diego Public Library. Dalton A. Degitz, Supervising Libn., Science & Industry Section. 820 E St., San Diego, **Calif.** 92101
Vols. 3000 Cat.

United Air Lines, Engineering Dept., Library. J. J. Whitney, Technical Libn. San Francisco International Airport, San Francisco, **Calif.** 94128
Vols. 4500 Cat.
Budget ($5500)
Notes: Mostly current books on technical aspects; some history books.

Hoover Institution on War, Revolution & Peace. Milorad M. Drachkovitch, Archivist. Stanford University, Stanford, **Calif.** 94305
Mss. Pix.

Notes: Papers of Radu Irimescu, Rumanian Minister of Air and Navy, 1932–38, and Rumanian Ambassador to the United States, 1938–40, incl. correspondence, reports, dispatches, memoranda, clippings, photos, and other material, 1918–40, relating to his service in the Rumanian government and to the development of aviation in Rumania. Primarily in Rumanian. 5 ms. boxes. Also, papers of Charles E. Weakley, Vice Admiral, U.S. Navy, commander, Antisubmarine Warfare Force, Atlantic Fleet, 1963–67, and assistant administrator for management development, National Aeronautics and Space Administration, 1968–72, incl. correspondence, orders, drafts of speeches, printed matter, photographs, and sound recordings, 1945–72, relating to post-World War II U.S. antisubmarine force operations and to NASA activities. 4 ms. boxes.

Denver Public Library. 1357 Broadway, Denver, **Colo.** 80203
Vols. 9000 Cat. Pix.
Notes: The Ross-Barrett Historical Aeronautics Collection. Aeronautics from the early myths through present space flight. The picture collection is heavily weighted with photos of planes used on the Western Front in the First World War though it does incl. other material. Do not purchase current technical material on airplane construction with the exception of homebuilts, but do purchase such materials up to about 1930. Many aeronautical periodicals are incl. in the collection.

U.S. Air Force Academy. Library. Benjamin C. Glidden. Dir. USAF Academy, **Colo.** 80840
Vols. 6000 Cat. Mss. Maps Pix
Notes: The Colonel Richard Gimbel Aeronautical History Collection. Incl. material from ancient myth to 1903 on manned flight, early scientific works on physical properties of the atmosphere, and imaginative literature on moon voyages. Collection is most complete in manned pioneer balloon ascents (1783ff). Also the Richard Upjohn Light Collection formerly at Culver Military Academy. Separate catalog, index to be published. 250 mss., 100 maps, 2000 pictures, 5000 prints, 7000 clippings.

Yale University Library. Manuscripts & Archives. Lawrence Dowler, Assoc. Libn. Box 1603A, Yale Sta. New Haven, **Conn.** 06520
Mss. Pix. Audiotapes Videotapes Microforms

Connecticut Aeronautical Historical Association. Bradley Air Museum Library. Robert Stepanek, Archivist; John W. Ramsay, Libn. Bradley International Airport. Windsor Locks, **Conn.** 06095
Mss. Maps Pix. Slides Phonorecords 16mm Films Filmstrips
Budget $2000

Air Transport Association of America. Library. Ms. Marion Mistrik, Libn. 1709 New York Ave. N.W., Washington, **D.C.** 20006
Vols. 14,000 Cat. Maps Pix. Microfilm
Budget $6000
Notes: Emphasis of collection is air transport, its history and economics. Incl. standard transportation texts, official administrative and statistical reports of the regulatory agencies, Congressional documents, annual reports of U.S. scheduled airlines, and a limited number of technical reports.

Smithsonian Institution Libraries. National Air & Space Museum Bureau. Catherine D. Scott, Bureau Libn. NASM Bldg., Sixth & Independence Ave., S.W., Washington, **D.C.** 20560
Vols. (22,000) Cat. Mss. Maps Pix. Slides Microforms
Notes: History of flight and aerospace development. incl. biographical material on aviation pioneers, balloons and ballooning. Extensive photographic collection (600,000 pictures). Incl. the Sherman Fairchild Collection of aeronautical photographs (transferred from the American Institute of Aeronautics and Astronautics). Also incl. the Bella Landauer

Aeronautical Sheet Music Collection (1500 pieces). 2000 films; 800,000 microforms; 4100 periodicals.

†Embry-Riddle Aeronautical University, Gill Robb Wilson Memorial Flight Center Library. M. Judy Luther, Dir. of Library Services. Regional Airport, Daytona Beach, **Fla.** 32015
Notes: Extensive new collection.

U.S. Naval Academy, Nimitz Library. Alice S. Creighton, Assistant Libn. for Special Collections. Annapolis, **Md.** 21402
Mss.
Notes: The William Adger Moffett Papers are a collection of official and personal letters, speeches, news releases, communications, memoranda, notes, news clippings, etc., by and about Rear Admiral William Adger Moffett, first Chief of the Bureau of Aeronautics, U.S. Navy. The collection is a primary source for any research regarding the early history of naval aviation. Papers relate to numerous topics, including the London Naval Treaty and its ramifications, military airships, United Air Service controversy, coastal defense, carriers, etc. Index is under preparation.

Johns Hopkins University, Milton S. Eisenhower Library, Special Collections. Charles & 34 Sts., Baltimore, **Md.** 21218
Cat. Mss. Pix. Audiotapes
Notes: Almost entirely a ms. collection. Personal papers, etc. 144 linear ft. Stephen Ferguson, Cur. of Rare Books. Princeton, N.J. 08540
Vols. 400 Cat. Pix.
Notes: The Harold McCormick Collection of early aeronautics.

State University of New York, Binghamton, Glenn G. Bartle Library. Ms. Marion Hanscom, Special Collections Libn. Binghamton, **N.Y.** 13901
Notes: A portion of the personal library of Edwin A. Link, pioneer in aeronautics, with his invention of the Link Trainer. This is a small collection of some 75 books dealing with aviation. The books augment an extensive collection of Link's papers.

Glenn H. Curtiss Museum of Local History. Merrill Stickler, Cur. Lake & Main Sts., Hammondsport, **N.Y.** 14840
Vols. 500 Uncat. Mss. Maps Pix. Slides Audiotapes 16mm Films Microforms
Budget $1000
Notes: The library may only be used by appointment by serious researchers. Some copying is allowed under special circumstances. Collection is basically concerned with Glenn H. Curtiss and his accomplishments in early aviation. Also collecting material about his contemporaries.

New York Public Library, Research Libraries. Robert G. Krupp, Chief, Science and Technology Research Center. Fifth Ave. & 42 St., New York, **N.Y.** 10018
Vols. (750,000) Cat. Microforms
Notes: Strong collection.

Dowling College. Library. John R. Beard, Dir. Idle Hour Blvd., Oakdale, **N.Y.** 11769
Vols. 500 Cat.
Budget $700

Cleveland Public Library. Helen Hauck, Head, Science & Technology Dept. 325 Superior Ave., Cleveland, **Ohio** 44114
Cat.
Notes: Notable segments in aeronautics, automobile engineering, and most other branches of engineering.

†Wright State University, Greater Miami Valley Research Center. Dayton, **Ohio** 45431

Ninety-Nines, Library. Dorothy Niekamp, Libn. P.O. Box 59964, Will Rogers World Airport, Oklahoma City, **Okla** 73159
Vols. 150 Cat. Pix.
Budget $700
Notes: Women in aviation.

Pennsylvania State University. Fred Lewis Pattee Library.
Charles Mann, Chief, Special Collections. University
Park, **Pa.** 16802
Vols. (122,533) Cat. Mss. Maps Pix. Slides
Phonorecords Audiotapes Videotapes 16mm Films
Microforms
Budget ($37,000)
Notes: Special Collections and Rare Books includes
several collections described separately. The holdings
are particularly strong in aeronautics.
DeGolyer Library, Southern Methodist University. Box
396. SMU Sta., Dallas, **Tex.** 75275
Vols. (90,000) Cat. Mss. Maps Pix. Slides Microforms
Washington State University Libraries, Manuscripts,
Archives, & Special Collections. John F. Guido. Head.
Pullman, **Wash.** 99164
Cat. Mss. Maps Pix.
Notes: The ms. collection incl personal and
professional papers of aviators. Described in *Selected
Manuscript Resources in the Washington State
University Library* (Pullman, 1974); and other published
and unpublished inventories and registers.
EAA Air Museum Foundation Research Library. Gene R.
Chase, Dir. P.O. Box 229, Hales Corners, **Wis.** 53130
Vols. 1500 Cat. Maps Pix. Slides Films Microforms
Notes: Mostly periodicals, engineering reports, aircraft
construction drawings, and other nonbook materials;
also about 1500 books, mostly textbooks and historical
works.
Centennial Planetarium. S. Wieser, Libn. P.O. Box 2100.
Calgary, Alta. T2P 2M5 **Can.**
Vols. (300) Uncat. Pix. Audiotapes 16mm Films
Notes: Also western Canadian aviation history with bias
towards technology; and history of space technology.
†National Museums of Canada Library. Audrey E. Dawe.
Chief, Library Services Div. Ottawa. Ont. K1A 0M8
Can.
Vols. 5650 Cat. Pix.
Notes: Historical aviation, stressing Canadian
contributions. The 10,000 pictures, with negatives, are
not part of the library: photos under supervision of
curator of National Museum of Science and
Technology. Prints may be ordered and used in
publication with credit to the National Museum of
Science and Technology.

AERONAUTICS—LAWS AND LEGISLATION
Air Transport Association of America, Library. Ms. Marion
Mistrik, Libn. 1709 New York Ave. N.W., Washington.
D.C. 20006
Vols. 14,000 Cat. Maps Pix. Microfilm
Budget $6000
Notes: Emphasis of collection is air transport, its history
and economics. Incl. standard transportation texts,
official administrative and statistical reports of the
regulatory agencies, Congressional documents, annual
reports of U.S. scheduled airlines, and a limited number
of technical reports.

AERONAUTICS—MEDICAL ASPECTS *see* Aviation
Medicine

AERONAUTICS—PHOTOGRAPHY *see* Photography.
Aerial

AERONAUTICS, COMMERCIAL
Stanford University Libraries. Florian J. Shasky, Libn.
Stanford, **Calif.** 94305
Vols. (1700) // Cat. Mss. Maps Pix.
Notes: The Timothy Hopkins Transportation Collection.
Some materials on aviation.
Air Transport Association of America, Library. Ms. Marion
Mistrik, Libn. 1709 New York Ave. N.W., Washington.
D.C. 20006

Vols. 14,000 Cat. Maps Pix. Microfilm
Budget $6000
Notes: Emphasis of collection is air transport, its history
and economics. Incl. standard transportation texts,
official administrative and statistical reports of the
regulatory agencies, Congressional documents, annual
reports of U.S. scheduled airlines, and a limited number
of technical reports.
United Airlines, Corporate Library. Constance G. Moore,
Corporate Libn. 1200 Algonquin Rd., P.O. Box 66100,
Chicago, **Ill.** 60666
Cat.
†Northwestern University, Transportation Center Library.
Mary Roy, Libn. Evanston, **Ill.** 60201
Vols. (58,700)
Notes: Air transportation.
Pan American World Airways, Corporate Library. Liwa
Chiu, Libn. 200 Park Ave., New York, **N.Y.** 10017
Vols. 450 Uncat. 16mm Films Microforms
Budget $2500
Notes: No photocopying.

AERONAUTICS, MILITARY
Claremont Colleges, Norman F. Sprague Memorial
Library. David Kuhner, Libn. 12 & Dartmouth,
Claremont, **Calif.** 91711
Vols. 3500 Cat. Mss. Maps Pix. Phonorecords
Notes: Gift of Rev. and Mrs. John F. B. Carruthers of
Pasadena, 1950. Emphasis on history of ballooning,
early aviation, World War I and World War II military
aviation, pioneer flyers and flights, women in aviation,
cartoons, songs, memorabilia, some diaries and
journals. Restricted use. Collection transferred here
from Honnold Library.
Northrop Corporation, Aircraft Group, Library Services
Dept. H. W. Jones, Manager. 3901 W. Broadway,
Hawthorne, **Calif.** 90250
Vols. (15,000) Cat. Microforms
Budget ($27,000)
Notes: Incl. file of military specifications and standards,
Air Force Technical Orders, and other military manuals,
handbooks, regulations, instructions, etc. Also 250,000
microfiche; 60,000 reports. Library use restricted to
employees; others by interlibrary loan.
U.S. Air Force Academy, Library. Benjaman C. Glidden,
Dir. USAF Academy, **Colo.** 80840
Vols. 3100 Cat. Mss. Microforms
U.S. Naval Academy, Nimitz Library. Alice S. Creighton,
Assistant Libn. for Special Collections. Annapolis, **Md.**
21402
Mss.
Notes: The William Adger Moffett Papers are a
collection of official and personal letters, speeches, notes,
news releases, communications, memoranda, notes,
news clippings, etc., by and about Rear Admiral William
Adger Moffett, first Chief of the Bureau of Aeronautics,
U.S. Navy. The collection is a primary source for any
research regarding the early history of naval aviation.
Papers relate to numerous topics, including the London
Naval Treaty and its ramifications, military airships,
United Air Service controversy, coastal defense,
carriers, etc. Index is under preparation.
82nd Airborne Div., War Memorial Museum, Reference
Library. Thomas M. Fairfull, Chief Cur. AFVCGE-M,
Ardennes & Gela Sts., Ft. Bragg, **N.C.** 28307
Vols. (300) Uncat. Mss. Maps Pix.
Notes: The collection is intended to be a research tool
for persons studying the history of the 82nd Airborne
Division and the development of airborne warfare.

AERONAUTICS, NAVAL *see* Aeronautics, Military

AERONAUTICS, WOMEN IN *see* Women in Aeronautics

AEROSPACE ENGINEERING

Rockwell International, Space Div., Technical Information Center. Barbara E. White, Libn. 12214 Lakewood Blvd., Downey, **Calif.** 90241
Vols. 48,000 Cat. Microforms
Notes: Primarily for use by company employees. Incl. journals and technical reports in the aerospace sciences and engineering; also 500,000 microforms

University of California, Los Angeles, Engineering & Mathematical Sciences Library. Rosalee I. Wright, Libn. 405 Hilgard, Los Angeles, **Calif.** 90024
Vols. (150,000) Cat. Microforms
Notes: See entry under Engineering.

NASA, Ames Research Center, Libraries. Ralph W. Lewis, Chief, Library Br. 202–3, Moffett Field, **Calif.** 94035
Vols. (70,000) Cat. Audiotapes Microforms
Budget ($260,000)
Notes: Main library collections cover physical sciences, engineering and mathematical fields related to research programs in aeronautics–space research. Life sciences library collections cover medical, physiological, behavioral and biological sciences related to research programs. Also emphasis on remote sensing of earth resources and the search for extraterrestrial life. 700 journal titles.

California State Polytechnic University, Pomona, University Library. Thomas L. Welch, Assoc. Dir. 3801 W. Temple Ave., Pomona, **Calif.** 91768
Vols. (23,000) Cat. Microforms
Budget ($40,000)
Notes: General Engineering Collection incl. aerospace, chemical, civil, electrical, electronics, industrial, mechanical and manufacturing engineering.

Georgia Institute of Technology, Price Gilbert Memorial Library. Edward Graham Roberts, Dir. 225 North Ave., Atlanta, **Ga.** 30332
Vols. (880,000) Cat. Maps Slides Microforms
Budget ($825,000)

Iowa State University, Library. Warren B. Kuhn, Dean of Library Services. Ames, **Iowa** 50011
Cat. Microforms
Notes: Extensive journal holdings.

†University of Kentucky, Robert E. Shaver Library of Engineering. Russell H. Powell, Engineering Libn. 355 Anderson Hall, Lexington, **Ky.** 40506
Vols. (29,660) Cat. Microforms

Boston University Libraries, Mugar Memorial Library. 771 Commonwealth Ave., Boston, **Mass.** 02215
Notes: Over 10,000 papers and reports from NASA, the Jet Propulsion Laboratory (California Institute of Technology), the armed services, etc. Gift of Allied Research Corp., Concord, Mass.

†Bendix Corp., Aerospace Systems Div., Technical Library. Valerie J. Edwards, Libn. 3300 Plymouth Rd., Ann Arbor, **Mich.** 48107
Vols. (3000) Cat.
Notes: Library has a well-rounded collection in applied technology with some pure science and an extension in the social sciences which has an additional 1000 books and a large collection of journals with a budget of approx. $5000. Also incl. 5000 documents, and 150,000 microfiche.

University of Michigan, Engineering-Transportation Library. Maurita Holland, Libn. 312 Undergraduate Library, Ann Arbor, **Mich.** 48104
Vols. (200,000) Cat. Microforms
Budget ($57,000)

Grumman Aerospace Corp., Technical Information Center. Royal Scheiman, Chief Libn. Plant 35, Bethpage, **N.Y.** 11714
Vols. 50,000 Cat. Microforms
Notes: Aerospace science and technology. Incl. 650,000 microforms.

American Institute of Aeronautics & Astronautics, Technical Information Service. Patricia Marshall, Chief Libn. 750 Third Ave., New York, **N.Y.** 10017
Vols. (57,000) Cat. Microforms
Notes: See entry under Aeronautics.

Schiele Museum of Natural History, Library. Dot Gray, Margaret Summerill, Libns. 1500 E. Garrison Blvd. Gastonia, **N.C.** 28052
Vols. (3800) Cat. Maps Pix. Slides Phonorecords Audiotapes 16mm Films Filmstrips Microforms
Budget ($2800)
Notes: Listed on RECON computer with Library of Congress as Reference Center in Southeast in subject areas of natural sciences, aerospace and planetarium technology, and anthropology.

North Carolina State University, D. H. Hill Library. I. T. Littleton, Dir. P.O. Box 50007, Raleigh, **N.C.** 27650
Vols. 6160 Cat.

University of Cincinnati, Engineering Library. Dorothy Furber Byers. Head. 849 Baldwin Hall, Cincinnati, **Ohio** 45221
Vols. (50,000) Cat. Videotapes Microforms
Budget ($57,000)

Franklin Institute Library. Emerson W. Hilker, Dir. 20 & The Parkway, Philadelphia, **Pa.** 19103
Vols. (300,000) Cat. Maps Pix. Microforms
Budget ($180,000)

University of Tennessee, Space Institute Library. Mrs. A. A. Mason, Research Facility Libn. Tullahoma, **Tenn.** 37388
Vols. (9000) Cat. Microforms
Notes: Incl. NASA and other series of technical reports.

University of Texas, Austin, General Libraries, Engineering Library. Jane Howell, Libn. P.O. Box P, Austin, **Tex.** 78712
Vols. (83,548) Cat. Microforms

General Dynamics/Fort Worth Div., Technical Library & Information Services. P. Roger de Tonnancour, Dir. P.O. Box 748, Mail Zone 2246, Fort Worth, **Tex.** 76101
Vols. 36,000 Cat. Maps Slides Microforms
Budget $100,000
Notes: Incl. 500,000 microforms. Catalogs for books and documents are separate. Collection is strong in mathematics, nuclear physics, materials and aerodynamics. Emphasis on the mission of the division—the development and production of manned aircraft. Division also involved in electronic manufacturing (avionic components), so collection strength in this area is growing very rapidly.

NASA-Langley Research Center, Technical Library. MS-185. Philip E. Weatherwax, Head, Tech. Library Branch. Hampton, **Va.** 23665
Vols. 55,000 Cat. Audiotapes Videotapes Microforms
Budget $230,000
Notes: Plus 22,000 vols. of bound journals; 200 audiotapes; 50 videotapes; 500,000 microforms; and 300,000 technical reports and documents. No photocopying.

AEROSPACE ENGINEERING—HISTORY

Smithsonian Institution Libraries, National Air & Space Museum Bureau. Catherine D. Scott, Bureau Libn. NASM Bldg., Sixth & Independence Ave., S.W., Washington, **D.C.** 20560
Vols. (22,000) Cat. Mss. Maps Pix. Slides Microforms
Notes: History of flight and aerospace development, incl. biographical material on aviation pioneers, balloons and ballooning. Extensive photographic collection (600,000 pictures). Incl. the Sherman Fairchild Collection of aeronautical photographs (transferred from the American Institute of Aeronautics and Astronautics). Also incl. the Bella Landauer Aeronautical Sheet Music Collection (1500 pieces). 2000 films; 800,000 microforms; 4100 periodicals.

AEROSPACE MEDICINE

U.S. Army, Aeromedical Research Laboratory, USAARL Library. Sybil H. Bullock, Libn. P.O. Box 577, Ft. Rucker, **Ala.** 36362
Vols. (30,000) Cat. Microforms
NASA, Ames Research Center, Libraries. Ralph W. Lewis, Chief, Library Br. 202-3, Moffett Field, **Calif.** 94035
Vols. (70,000) Cat. Audiotapes Microforms
Budget ($260,000)
Notes: Main library collections cover physical sciences, engineering and mathematical fields related to research programs in aeronautics–space research. Life sciences library collections cover medical, physiological, behavioral and biological sciences related to research programs. Also emphases on remote sensing of earth resources and the search for extraterrestrial life. 700 journal titles.
Civil Aero Medical Institute Library (CAMI). Darrell R. Goulden, Medical Libn. P.O. Box 25082, Oklahoma City, **Okla.** 73125
Vols. 8500 Cat. Mss.
Budget $28,000
Notes: Aviation and aerospace medicine. About 350 current periodicals.
U.S. Air Force School of Aerospace Medicine, Strughold Aeromedical Library. Fred W. Todd, Chief Libn. Brooks AFB, **Tex.** 78235
Vols. 111,000 Cat. Mss. Maps Pix. Microforms
Notes: Material not oriented to the School of Aerospace Medicine are excluded. Incl. also 37,000 microforms and 92,000 technical documents.

AEROSPACE SCIENCES—HISTORY

Smithsonian Institution Libraries, National Air & Space Museum Bureau. Catherine D. Scott, Bureau Libn. NASM Bldg., Sixth & Independence Ave., S.W., Washington, D.C. 20560
Vols. (22,000) Cat. Mss. Maps Pix. Slides Microforms
Notes: History of flight and aerospace development, incl. biographical material on aviation pioneers, balloons and ballooning. Extensive photographic collection (600,000 pictures). Incl. the Sherman Fairchild Collection of aeronautical photographs (transferred from the American Institute of Aeronautics and Astronautics). Also incl. the Bella Landauer Aeronautical Sheet Music Collection (1500 pieces). 2000 films; 800,000 microforms; 4100 periodicals.

AEROSTATION see Aeronautics

ASTRONAUTICS

University of California, Los Angeles, Engineering & Mathematical Sciences Library. Rosalee I. Wright, Libn. 405 Hilgard, Los Angeles, **Calif.** 90024
Vols. (150,000) Cat. Microforms
Notes: Library collects in the fields of engineering, astronomy, mathematics, and meteorology. NACA and NASA report series and NASA microfiche depository of technical reports (inclusive); AAS publications (inclusive); AIAA journals and selected AIAA conference publications; AIAA papers on microfiche (1969–1974).
Purdue University Libraries/AVC, Engineering Library. Edwin D. Posey, Engineering Libn. A. A. Potter Engineering Center, W. Lafayette, **Ind.** 47907
Vols. (117,301) Cat. Maps Audiotapes Microforms
Budget ($152,473)
University of Massachusetts/Amherst Libraries, Physical Sciences Library. Vlasta K. Greenbie, Head. Amherst, **Mass.** 01003
Vols. (108,000) Cat. Microforms
Notes: Incl. extensive holdings of journals, NACA and NASA publications, and AEC documents (microfiche).
†Smithsonian Institution Libraries, Astrophysical Observatory Branch. Joyce Rey, Libn. 60 Garden St.,

Cambridge, **Mass.** 02138
Vols. (10,000) Cat. Maps Pix. Microforms
Princeton University Library. Jean Preston, Cur. Princeton, **N.J.** 08540
Cat. Mss. Maps Pix.
Notes: Incl. the collection of G. Edward Pendray detailing the entry of the United States into the space age; much on early rocketry and the work of Richard H. Goddard. Tape recordings and motion pictures incl. Described in *Wilson Library Bulletin*, March 1968.
American Institute of Aeronautics & Astronautics, Technical Information Service. Patricia Marshall, Chief Libn. 750 Third Ave., New York, **N.Y.** 10017
Vols. (57,000) Cat. Microforms
Notes: Basis of published literature input to NASA Information System; Special index—Semimonthly issues of *International Aerospace Abstracts* with cumulated semiannual and annual indexes.
American Museum–Hayden Planetarium, Richard S. Perkin Library. Sandra Kitt, Libn. 81 St. & Central Park W., New York, **N.Y.** 10024
Vols. (15,000) Cat. Maps Pix. Slides
Budget ($5000)
Notes: Considered one of the strongest and most complete astronomy libraries on the east coast. Contains the Bliss Collection of Ancient Astronomical Instruments; also the Mt. Wilson/Bloman Sky Survey to the 45 degree declination; the Lick Observatory Survey; *American Ephemeris and Nautical Almanac*, 1855-date.
Franklin Institute Library. Emerson W. Hilker, Dir. 20 & The Parkway, Philadelphia, **Pa.** 19103
Vols. (300,000) Cat. Maps Pix. Microforms
Budget ($180,000)

ASTRONAUTICS—BIOGRAPHY

Smithsonian Institution Libraries, National Air & Space Museum Bureau. Catherine D. Scott, Bureau Libn. NASM Bldg., Sixth & Independence Ave., S.W., Washington, D.C. 20560
Vols. (22,000) Cat. Mss. Maps Pix. Slides Microforms
Notes: History of flight and aerospace development, incl. biographical material on aviation pioneers, balloons and ballooning. Extensive photographic collection (600,000 pictures). Incl. the Sherman Fairchild Collection of aeronautical photographs (transferred from the American Institute of Aeronautics and Astronautics). Also incl. the Bella Landauer Aeronautical Sheet Music Collection (1500 pieces). 2000 films; 800,000 microforms; 4100 periodicals.

ASTRONAUTICS—HISTORY

†San Diego Public Library. Dalton A. Degitz, Supervising Libn., Science & Industry Section. 820 E St., San Diego, **Calif.** 92101
Vols. 3000 Cat.
Smithsonian Institution Libraries, National Air & Space Museum Bureau. Catherine D. Scott, Bureau Libn. NASM Bldg., Sixth & Independence Ave., S.W. Washington, D.C. 20560
Vols. (22,000) Cat. Mss. Maps Pix. Slides Microforms
Notes: History of flight and aerospace development, incl. biographical material on aviation pioneers, balloons and ballooning. Extensive photographic collection (600,000 pictures). Incl. the Sherman Fairchild Collection of aeronautical photographs (transferred from the American Institute of Aeronautics and Astronautics). Also incl. the Bella Landauer Aeronautical Sheet Music Collection (1500 pieces). 2000 films; 800,000 microforms; 4100 periodicals.
Johns Hopkins University, Milton S. Eisenhower Library, Special Collections. Charles & 34 Sts., Baltimore, **Md.** 21218
Cat. Mss. Pix. Audiotapes
Notes: Almost entirely a ms. collection. Personal

XIII

Proposing or Dragon Kissing IV

A Brilliant Ph.D. in Art History, a specialist in medieval art, wrote a dissertation on Classical Themes in Medieval Tapestry. The five fashionable garments:

Cape: Electrical wiring, design and installation of lighting fixtures; coordinating antipathetic business elements; balancing impossible loads.

Gown: Businessmen, shops, antiques.

Boots and *Spurs:* A radical change of family fortune from student poverty to a stockbroker's munificence, thanks to beloved spouse's excellent job in a New York suburb, thus requirement to stay within commuting distance of the Big Apple. ("This is a cataclysm?" you ask. Lady Justine answers, "Surprise! Not all cataclysms are negative.")

Spectacles: Ruins, fragments, historic buildings.

Cap: Loves stability, within reason, but also the thrill and excitement of the unknown; has a violent hatred of waste.

This is the same Brilliant Ph.D. we encountered earlier, in Chapter X, *Correlating* (or *Dragon Kissing* I) who, once prodded, produced fascinating business capabilities via the practical electrical engineering company, installing domestic and commercial lighting fixtures. Clearly this art historian has a strong entrepreneurial bent.

The Template:

An administrative position combining business with the arts and humanities, emanating from either the academic or mercantile side, but creatively serving the purposes of each. A commercial art gallery's

education program or an auction house might be a suitable site, or a college or a group of colleges requiring business degree programs.

The Brilliant Ph.D. did extensive research in unlikely colleges, educational programs in cultural institutions, and enterprising projects in business; reviewed the file cards carefully; talked with friends and acquaintances. Clear thinking yielded these several conclusions:

1. Many colleges have business courses but almost none connect business with the humanities and the arts, with the exception of a few specialized arts management programs stressing more management than art.

2. Liberal arts colleges wishing to offer more business courses cannot afford to hire new faculty even though these courses and faculty might attract necessary new students.

3. Many businesses have educational programs but usually exclusively for their own employees and for their own subjects.

4. Students who might love the arts and humanities do not study them because of the justifiable fear of post-graduate unemployment.

5. Faculties at most liberal arts colleges are seriously imperiled because few registered students mean few courses in the humanities specialties, and the possible firings even of tenured faculty by direct abolition of departments or administrative reorganization.

6. Certain liberal arts colleges, particularly a group of small private institutions on the Hudson River, suffer severely and absurdly. Desperate for students, the colleges nevertheless have several potential likely clienteles immediately nearby. One is older intelligent suburban women who want to complete interrupted degrees, or get master's degrees in humanistic subjects likely to allow professional practice later on. A second is traditional college age people whose middle class parents want the indulgence of liberal arts education yet the applicable utility of learning after graduation, namely the seemingly impossible combination of luxury and practicality.

7. Something has to be done. Someone has to do it.

The Brilliant Ph.D. first addressed the problems of those liberal arts colleges on the Hudson River since location was important because of the suburban stockbroker spouse, the *Boots of Restriction* and *Spurs of Incentive*. Applying the Rotation process to certain of those colleges' problems, the Brilliant Ph.D. perceived that Hudson River Colleges located in the exurbs of New York City were fortunate to be so near cultural delights of the city yet so far from its dirt and crime, therefore perfect for trips in but living out. Someone or something should be able to lure students to them. Mere public relations programs surely would not do. Substantial programs suiting students' needs most likely would. If the Brilliant Ph.D. could sell such an idea to the colleges which thereby could increase their enrollments and their financial coffers, they might hire the Brilliant Ph.D. to run the program.

Hallelujah! They did. The proposal, cleverly playing on the conventional MBA or Master in Business Administration, was titled: *The NBA: The New Business Alternative in the Arts and Humanities.*

NBA
The New Business Alternative in the Arts and Humanities

For invigorating the arts, humanities, and social sciences

For vivifying language learning
(and integrating English as a Second Language students)

For assuring student employment

For revitalizing demoralized faculty

CONTAINING

I

NBA WHEEL OF TRAINING
What It Is, Why, and How It Works

NBA, the New Business Alternative in the Arts and Humanities, is an undergraduate degree or certificate allowing immediate application of humanities, arts, and social science majors to the American and international commercial worlds. In addition to their strong backgrounds in traditional disciplines, NBA graduates will possess marketable skills in professions currently strong in employment and likely to remain so. Both students and parents ought to delight in such prospect.

An NBA is possible in every discipline in the arts and humanities and most particularly in social sciences. Following are examples of professions an NBA graduate is equipped to enter.

NBA IN ART: art galleries; corporate art purchasing; international art auctions.

NBA IN MUSIC: management of performers, groups, orchestras, concert halls, recording studios, and international variations thereof.

NBA IN HISTORY: local and international historic preservation projects; foreign and domestic travel promotion; foreign and domestic market research.

NBA IN FOREIGN LANGUAGES: international merchandising, multinational corporations; publishing of foreign language magazines and books.

NBA IN ENGLISH: literary agencies; advertising, representation of American or foreign publishers; editing and commercial management for publishers of books, magazines, newspapers, and specialty journals.

NBA IN MEDIEVAL AND RENAISSANCE STUDIES: educational and public programs at museums and cultural centers; promotion, advertising, and public relations for schools and universities.

NBA IN PSYCHOLOGY: local and international sports medicine; motivational coaching for sports in schools, recreation facilities, and international competitions; corporate executive fitness and worker well-being programs; counseling in diet centers.

GBA, the Graduate Business Alternative in the Arts and Humanities, is a graduate version of the NBA for professionals in the arts and humanities.

The Wheel of Training for the NBA and GBA consists of 33 credits:
1.   Required Hub Courses for all students in the program (24 credits);
2.   Selected Spokes Courses for the particular discipline or department (9 credits);
3.   Obligatory Rim Course for all students (no credit).

The responsibilities of the college or university to the NBA program are to:
1.   Recognize that the ulterior motives for the NBA are to provide intellectually valuable and academically sound employment options for students and a salvation scheme for college and university humanities programs throughout the nation.
2.   Create the new curriculum: new courses integrating the best of traditional knowledge with a practical format as *addition to,* not replacement for, traditional departmental majors; and with a strong international, therefore foreign language, bias.
3.   Retrain the humanities faculty in existing departments for tutelage in the new curriculum.
4.   Hire adjunct or more permanent business experts to retrain faculty and teach the *Spokes* courses..
5.   Establish a professional placement office for Spokes apprenticeships and career appointments.

II

NBA HUB COURSES
24 credits required of all NBA and GBA students

NBA MATH (3 credits)
Includes statistics, descriptive and inferential; basic accounting procedures; budgets; five-year projections; double entry bookkeeping; numerical probability; inventory tallying; cost-effect ratios; foreign currency conversion; basic economic theory; supply and demand theory and practice.

NBA ENGLISH (3 credits)

Includes rhetoric; grammar; logical exposition; propaganda; reports; correspondence; scenarios; proof reading and copy editing; literary property rights; copyrights; press releases; data summaries; short remarks.

NBA SEDUCTION ARTS (3 credits)

Includes public speaking; dramatic presentation; case proofs; rhetorical aggression and defense; consumer convincing; merchandise display; advertising layout and paste up; ear appeal versus eye appeal versus truth; integration of Marvelous Machines (see below) such as slides and film clips to enhance oral persuasion.

NBA FOREIGN LANGUAGE (12 credits; no excuses)

The goal is to achieve suitably utilitarian competence in speaking, reading, and writing the language for its employment in international business correspondence, diplomacy, negotiations, travel, and decision making.

Four full semesters are required.

Semester 1 FFF—Food, Fashion, and Flying.
Three universally interesting subjects no matter what the student's specialty.

Semester 2 DDD—Diplomacy, Dogma, and Dirty Tricks.
Includes readings from Machiavelli through Watergate.

Semester 3 PST—Persevering and Surviving or Thriving.
Practical dramatic scenarios for business and commerce as: the first sale; the double-cross; drunk at the helm; the boss' wife or Potiphar's wife revisited; descent into the sewers of Paris or Milan or Madrid or Quito.

Semester 4—Identical to NBA English, but in the foreign language.

New Methods of Instruction.

1. Bilingual Texts. Foreign and English languages presented on facing pages, immersing the students in the substance first and the mechanics second; utilization of mostly modern materials from newspapers, periodicals, and trade journals.

2. Buddy System. The English speaking student studying Spanish or French or Chinese is paired with a native speaker learning English as a Second Language, who gives oral practice and introductory cultural background. A special lounge provides access to a record collection, rack of popular English and foreign publications, and required foreign films.

3. Two Ulpans. Imitating the successful Israeli technique called the Ulpan, for teaching immigrants functional, frill-less Hebrew, the NBA

and GBA require two one-week morning-till-night "house arrest" incarcerations and total immersions in the language during winter or spring vacations at the end of semesters 2 and 4.

NBA MARVELOUS MACHINES (3 credits)
The goal is to develop facility with the major business machines. Ten necessaries are: typewriter (attain accurate 40 wpm); calculator; Telex; word processor; computer, including introduction to keyboard, console, print-out, reader, languages such as Basic and Elementary Fortran; inventory recorders; microphones; slide projectors; film strips; closed circuit television; electronic and ultrasonic surveillance and security systems including bugs and tapes.

III

NBA SPOKES COURSES
9 credits to be selected according to the student's NBA or GBA major.

Three single-semester 3-credit courses will be taken according to three special structures: (1) substance, (2) style, and (3) apprentice employment.

NBA IN ART (9 credits)
Three courses in gallery art in conjunction with major Manhattan art galleries and auction houses such as Sotheby Parke Bernet, Phillips, and Christie's. Includes period styles in works of art and furniture; dating; appraisal; pricing; authenticity and forgery; vagaries of the art market; customer relations; corporate art investments; displays; sales; records; catalogue writing; advertising and promotion; art and display reviews; liaisons with museums, other corporations, and collectors; basic restoration techniques; basic international art law concerning antiques, national treasures, smuggling, and rights of return; international amenities in the art market (Sotheby Parke Bernet, for example, has branches in Canada, Scotland, South Africa, Switzerland, France, Belgium, Holland, Mexico, Brazil, North Africa, and India).

NBA IN ENGLISH (9 credits)
Three courses in conjunction with major New York City literary agencies such as Scott Meredith; publishers such as Charles Scribner's Sons,

Crown, Harper & Row, George Braziller; trade journals such as *Stores* (merchandising) and *Lithopinion* (printers union). Includes professional and specialized readership versus intelligent popular readership; basic publishing law and strategy as in contracts, copyrights, permissions, foreign co-editions; acquisitions; basic technical writing; editing, copy editing, manuscript preparation; deadlines; book and magazine design and layout; basic production, as methods of printing and binding, hot, cold and electronic typesetting systems, preparations for printing; foreign language translations and foreign book markets; literary promotion of trade, text, and juvenile books.

NBA IN THEATER ARTS (9 credits)
Three courses in association with The Schubert Organization, Chal Associates, Al Pacino, and Actors Equity. Includes arts management of individuals, groups, or theaters; bookings; tours; solo appearances; gigs; promotions; profits versus risks; timing; coaching; professional unions; house management and box office; stage management and back stage; technical direction, lighting, scenic design and construction; theatrical para-medicine; criticism and reviews; theater as industry; entertainment law, contracts, rights, and liabilities; theater financing, accounting, budgeting, and fund-raising.

IV

NBA RIM COURSE
No credit but required of all NBA and GBA students

ETHICS OF THE MARKET PLACE
Establishes equilibrium between philosophical questions and practical answers. Includes morality versus profit; quality versus quantity; cost versus risk; worker and consumer safety versus plant overhead; ecology versus commerce; the job versus the life; work versus leisure; pleasure versus paycheck; truth versus expediency; foreign customs versus American amenities; gift versus bribe; education versus sedition; the business idea versus the business reality.

V

CONCLUSION

The NBA, the New Business Alternative in the Arts and Humanities, and the GBA, the Graduate Business Alternative in the Arts and Humanities, afford:

    1. Utilitarian skills for a primary profession in the arts and humanities;

    2. Marketable skills in case of expansion of or retrenchment from the primary profession, allowing a dependable secondary or fall-back profession.

This is an all-exigency program serving just as do the "engine-out" procedures in aviation. One hopes never to endure a failed engine at 4000 feet above ground level. But one learns the practical procedures, and practices them, for readiness to meet the professional perils.

VI

EPILOGUE
Who is so Stupid as to Pay $48,000 to Rent a Hat?
or
Some Painful Truths Revealed

The humanities never were pure. Rarely were they studied for "their own sake." They were always preprofessional, for medicine, law, education, or business.

The humanities never were popular. Language studies, for example, thrived not so much by inherent desirability but because they were required. Students of yore having no mystical sense of Latin's utility simply could not get their degrees without it. Ergo classics flourished. Some students introduced under duress stayed for love. But those with flair hoped to follow their professors professionally into the academic fields, an option no longer possible. Requirements, not allure, made for the humanities' past paper popularity.

The Parents' Plight. Parents of all social classes dare not afford useless luxury. Who is so stupid as to pay $48,000 to rent a mortarboard? Parents are not willing to encourage their progeny's humanities majors fitting them for little more than wearing the rented hat at graduation. Even people intellectually committed to humanistic endeavor cannot invest in ephemera. A Full Professor's annual salary of $46,000, before taxes, does not cover a daughter's $14,000 college bill plus a son's $12,700, and another $1,750 each for miscellaneous travel, clothes, books, bicycle repairs, and summer feeding. An attorney making $95,000 has only a few thousand more in take home pay than the professor, after the legal assistants, secretaries, and office rentals are covered. An orthopedic surgeon earning $185,000 not only has office overhead and higher tax bracket to contend with but astronomical malpractice insurance premiums, nonreturnable and payable yearly, allowing little ready cash for education. All three sets of parents would encourage intellectual experimentation and intelligent indulgence in the humanities but their children must have an after-college potential for self-support. If such professional parents question conventional humanities and arts programs how much more so the "first generation" college parents with no tradition for intellectual arts other than suspicious hostility. For them the child's education is the ladder to higher social class by earned income. All parents of college age people, as well as those students living on personal income, require a practical, easily established, bureaucratically simple alternative to the "Liberal Arts": the New Business Alternative in the Arts and Humanities, and the Graduate Business Alternative in the Arts and Humanities.

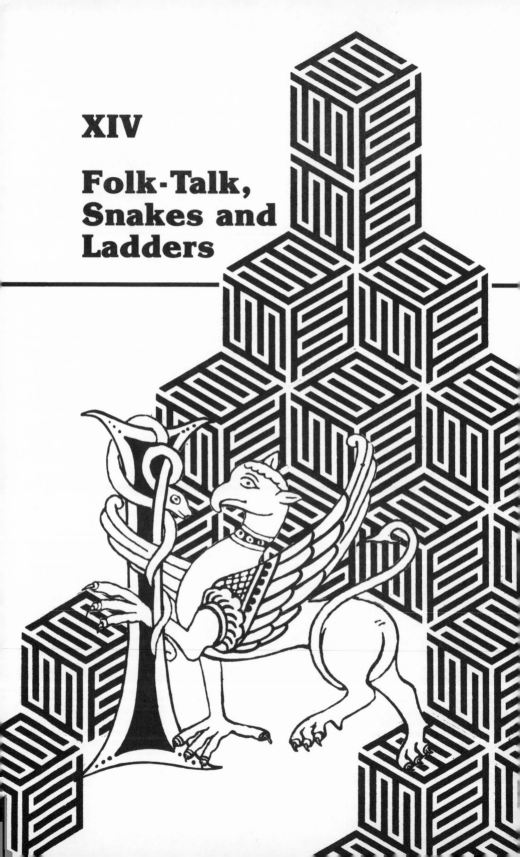

XIV

Folk-Talk, Snakes and Ladders

This fine proposal worked like magic. It was designed with care, sparked by cleverness, and presented with clarity. These three Cs are essential to plans that work. However, the project would not have been proposed nor accepted if not for Folk-Talk, snakes, and ladders.

Folk-Talk is Lady Justine's insistence upon your speaking with various people about your project or your plans at least four times every day. Each conversation must be with a different intelligent person totally dissociated from your current circle of friends. Ideally, you ought to speak with strangers in unexpected places: a waitress, a taxi driver, a man at the laundromat, a bookstore manager, a building janitor.

"Folk-Talk!" you exclaim. "It is nonsense to converse with utter strangers about important problems. What do they know? How can they help? Folk-Talk seems ridiculous." "Certainly not," answers Lady Justine. "Folk know more than you think." The man running the copy machine reproducing your resume is a writer with connections to Pittsburgh public television and radio stations as well as with six film magazines for which he writes. His ideas lead to the concepts and the names in the "New Business Alternative in English" section of the proposal, as well as to his roommate, an actor between shows, whose girlfriend, a documentary producer, knows most of the local experimental film makers. One invites you to a screening where you meet a man notable for his lion's mane of white hair under which he hides his head as director of the State Council on the Arts which funds projects like yours. Though

107

his budget for this year is committed, he personally knows the director of the National Endowment for the Humanities Education Division for Regional and National Grants which is looking for precisely such programs as the *NBA* to invigorate humanistic studies with practical applications.

Your building janitor is uneducated but wise and does free-lance carpentry for the owner of an audio-electronics firm, which in addition to selling stereo components also supports arts programs at Lincoln Center. Just this chance encounter leads to a promise of employment for the students who will people the program which does not yet exist. However, he gives you the inspiration for the employment section of your proposal as well as an introduction to the development officer at Lincoln Center who thinks your idea superior and wants to integrate part of it into his own fund-raising plans for the symphony and the opera.

"Stop," shouts Lady Justine. "That snake just became a ladder." "What in heaven . . ." you begin. "No," interrupts Lady Justine, "Not in heaven. Snakes move gracefully on earth. They slither silently in serpentine motion below eye level on the ground, through tall grass, burrowing under barriers to the other side. Seeming to move in partial circles, they efficiently traverse point to point. Where noisy direct action might fail, snakes surreptitiously succeed."

"Ladders are used for climbing up. Ladders permit scaling over barriers. At least they help raise you high enough

to see to the other side. Ladders, almost always upright, on the way up, encourage climbing."

"But," you begin, sputtering, "surely you are not, that is, you cannot make the preposterous comparison between acquaintances and snakes, or helpers and ladders."

"Certainly," answers Lady Justine. "You have a misapprehension of those magnificent limbless reptiles. Furthermore, your childhood must have been deprived if you never played that fine board game called 'Snakes and Ladders.' Never mind. This is analogy not substance. Think of all acquaintances to whom you Folk-Talk as bees. Busily buzzing, they carry pollen from flower to flower to fertilize them, while they themselves, collecting nectar, produce honey and wax. Beeswax candles and honey to eat make true sweetness and light."

Folk-Talk also forces you to an uncommon clarity of ideas and direct facility for expressing them. When you must explain a project quickly to an intelligent though unlearned listener you reduce complexity to essentials. You use vivid unambiguous vocabulary. You avoid misinterpretable language. If your Template, for example, suggests an important interreligious educational position with the American Council of Churches or similar ecclesiastical consortium, you tentatively title your project, "Magnificence of Traditional Jewry." Folk-Talk. Your listeners hear "Jewry" as Jewelry and for several minutes think you are a silver

craftsman not a doctor of comparative religion. Folk-Talk forces you to change the title to one that scintillates clearly.

Folk-Talk also generates care, cleverness, and clarity in ordering ideas. Intelligent folk think adverbially. They classify the new according to its how, when, where, and why. In fact, scholars and scientists and folk are adverb lovers. Not so attorneys and judges who march to a different grammar, demanding discrete nouns and verbs: precisely who did exactly what. Not so artists who are adjectivers, creating variations upon beauty, age, goodness, and size. Folk-Talking scholars thinking and speaking adverbially, easily create winning proposals by ordering them adverbially.

> Why is the project needed?
> How can it be accomplished?
> Where can it thrive?
> When can it begin?

At the end of the proposal, the obvious name of "who" can perform the action is added so that the result, a contract for your employment, becomes inevitable.

"How" is a tricky adverb, though, usually translating into the question "However will we pay for it?" That introduces the subject of grantsmanship for which several fine books exist. Your own ingenuity or a good librarian will direct you through them. Your proposal, however, according to your Template should be so compelling that it will fit an existing budget line in the particular unlikely university, or educational division of a cultural institution, or the business or corporation requiring your enterprising plan.

That is not dependence upon magic. Reason and experience suggest that if you offer a service useful to the organization for which you, because of your Template, are the only and sterlingly qualified candidate, you will get a job to perform that service. The title may not be exactly as your Template formulates it. "Never mind title," says Lady Justine. "Concentrate on work with SARAH." "What does the Biblical matriarch have to do with my profession?" you ask. "Everything," Lady Justine replies. "The whole purpose of ingenious packaging of talents and predilections is SARAH: SAlary, Reward, And Hope.

Postscript

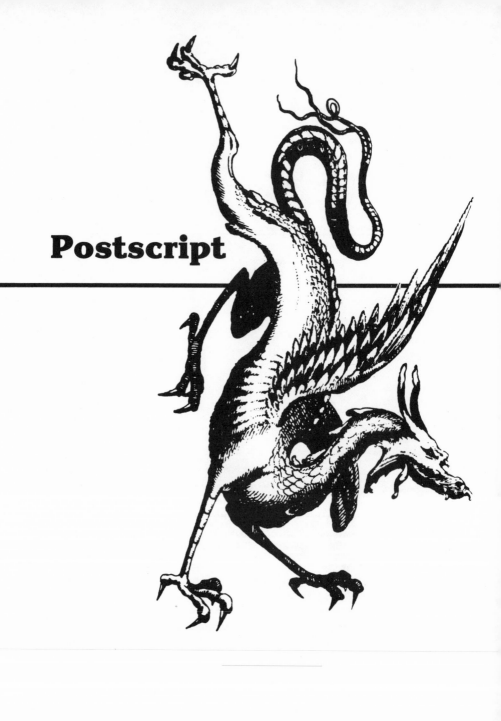

This book's case histories of Brilliant Ph.D.s whose ingenious packaging of talents and predilections led to fine positions are all true to fact, but details are slightly disguised to protect privacy. Ingenious packaging is somewhat like plastic surgery. Some people with a radiant new nose or new position, while grateful to the practitioner for the transformation, prefer to think of the new beauty as always having been and ever more shall be. However, I hear that tee-shirts and tote-bags with portraits of Lady Justine have been seen in California, Michigan, Massachusetts, and New York State. I myself have seen two joggers in Central Park with Lady Justine on their chests. Those tiny gold dragon pins seen occasionally on shirt collars and lapels are sported by devotees of Lady Justine so we can recognize one another in a crowd.

Share Your Success with *Kissing the Dragon*

We keep files of successful work-hunters' achievements. If you wish to share your experiences, write to us with details. Be sure to include your

Cape of Competence
Gown of Compatibility
Boots of Restriction and *Spurs of Incentive*
Spectacles of Suitability
Cap of Abstraction.

Then give us the title and brief description of your
JOB.

Also if you have suggestions or corrections you would hope to see in the next edition of *Kissing the Dragon,* you are welcome to write to us at:

BARD HALL PRESS
32 Knickerbocker Road
Tenafly, New Jersey 07670

Gratitude

Hundreds of people courageously have endured *Kissing the Dragon*. I honor their achievements. In the preceding chapters, I described their problems and resolutions, but I disguised particular details to protect their privacy. While those intelligent work-hunters must be anonymous, other friends' names merit mention: Professor David Riesman at Harvard; Dr. Bern Dibner of the Burndy Library; Dr. Millicent Carey McIntosh, former President of Barnard College; at the University of California at San Diego, Dr. Ronald Berman; at *Time* magazine, Dr. Roger Rosenblatt; at City University of New York, Provosts Harry Lustig and Linda Mantel, Professor Conrad and Lore Schirokauer of City College; President Leonard Lief of Lehman College, and Dr. Gertrude Schneider and Dr. Roberta Thornton of the Graduate Center; at Columbia Presbyterian Medical Center, President Michael Sovern, Dr. John Kingsley Lattimer, Dr. Andrew Gibson Frantz, Miss Kathy Armstrong, Bard Clifford Cosman, Rebecca Kurth, Drs. Dewitt and Anne Goodman.

At Bergen Community College of New Jersey, Dean Lois Marshall and Lenore Weisenfeld; at the University of Western Michigan, Professor Otto Grundler and Dr. Audrey Davidson; at the University of Toronto, Dr. Ruth Pelner Donnelly; at Fairleigh Dickinson University, Professors Wallace McMullen, Gilbert Steiner, Julius Luck, and Stella Esrig; Samuel Convissor (RCA Corporation), Roger Etherington (Horizon Corporation) and Henry Becton (Becton-Dickinson Corporation); at the Medieval Festival Guild of New York, Bob Isaac, Helen Churko, Dr. Albert Blumberg; at *Helicon Nine,* Kansas City, Missouri, Gloria Vando Hickok; and good friends in New York and New Jersey: Dr. William Ober, Patricia Symonds, Douglas Golde, Henry Westphalen, Rozlyn Chelouche, Barbara Sasoon, the Very Reverend James Park Morton, Stewart Mott, Lillian Lenane, Carole Brock, Irena Chalmers, Ann McGavin, Rabbi Arthur Hertzberg, New Jersey State Senator Matthew Feldman, Phyllis Kriegel, Elinore Wharton, Dr. J.J. Keyser, New York Councilman Stanley Michaels, and Dr. and Mrs. Louis Pelner.

Preparing and refining the manuscript with me were Tom Lang, Alexa Pierce, Robert Zoller, Susan Urstadt, and Anna-

Marie Scopelitto-Olsen. Bard Hall Press and I are particularly grateful for permissions to reproduce illustrations from the Dover Pictorial Archive Series. Especially important have been the volumes:

Alphabets and Ornaments by Ernst Lehner.

Art Deco Designs and Motifs, rendered by Marcia Loeb.

Curious Woodcuts of Fanciful and Real Beasts, by Konrad Gesner.

Decorative Alphabets and Initials, edited by Alexander Nesbitt.

Designs and Patterns from Historic Ornament, by W. and G. Audsley.

Historic Alphabets and Initials: Woodcut and Ornamental, edited by Carol Belanger Grafton.

Pictorial and Decorative Title Pages from Music Sources, selected by Gottfried S. Fraenkel.

Picture Sourcebook for Collage and Decoupage, edited by Edmund V. Gillon, Jr.

Symbols, Signs, and Signets, by Ernst Lehner.

Treasury of Art Nouveau Design and Ornament, selected by Carol Belanger Grafton.

Details from prints, engravings, and woodcuts have been derived from illustrations in the collections of the Metropolitan Museum of Art, the Morgan Library, and Galeria Medievalia. Thanks for friendship in need must be credited to Miss M. McCarthy for the several pages derived from Ash's *Subject Collections,* 5th Edition, with permission of the R. R. Bowker Company. Copyright © 1978 by Xerox Corporation.

The Dragon appearing on the cover, title page, p. 16, and the postscript page is from E. Edwards and M. Darly, *A New Book of Chinese Designs Calculated to Improve the Present Taste . . . ,* London, 1754, which we reproduce thanks to the gracious permission of the Walters Art Gallery, Baltimore; Avery Library, Columbia University; and Galeria Medievalia, New York and London.

Bard Hall Press handled this volume with accustomed competence and affection for beautiful books: Janet Czarnetzki, Art Director; Sheree Bykofsky Production Editor; and Marin Cosman, Managing Editor; Henry Iken and Bob Walters of Walken Graphics, typographers, and John D. Grady of John D. Lucas Company, Baltimore, printers.

The ultimate thanks are the Dedication.

Other Books by Madeleine Pelner Cosman

Fabulous Feasts: Medieval Cookery and Ceremony
New York: George Braziller, 1976; paperback, 1978
Nominated for Pulitzer Prize and National Book Award

Machaut's World: Science and Art in the Fourteenth Century
New York: New York Academy of Sciences, 1978

Medieval Holidays and Festivals: A Calendar of Celebrations
New York: Charles Scribner's Sons, 1981

The Education of the Hero in Arthurian Romance
Oxford, and Chapel Hill: University of North Carolina Press, 1966

The Letterbook of Marvelous Beasts: An Alliterative Alphabet
Tenafly, New Jersey: Bard Hall Press, 1984

Forthcoming Bard Hall Books

The Medieval Food of Love
The Medieval Jewish Gourmet: A Maimonidean Cookbook
Medieval Jewish Life and Love
Dictionary of the Medieval World
Business Women in the Middle Ages
Medieval Splendor: Daily Living in Castle and Cottage
End with a Bang: The Intelligent Physician's Guide to Retiring and
        Selling the Practice

If these titles intrigue you, write for our catalogue.

BARD HALL PRESS
32 Knickerbocker Road
Tenafly, New Jersey 07670

More Dragons

Those who share a difficult labor and a triumph not only grow fond of one another but of the agony that unites them. Graduates of *Kissing the Dragon* usually proudly wear their gold dragon pins. Many also have requested our whimsical handsome T-shirts and chef's aprons. If you have endured the perils and pleasures of *Kissing the Dragon* and wish to celebrate it, then you are welcome to order:

Kissing the Dragon shirts, at $5.00 each, available as:
green dragon on black shirt (GRN)
crimson dragon on grey shirt (CRM)
in Small (S), Medium (M), Large (L), and Extra Large (XL),
and
Kissing the Dragon chef's aprons, at $10.00 each
in one universal size.

· ·

Your Name _____

Address _____

City _____

State _____ Zip Code _____

	Quantity	Size (S,M,L,XL)	Color (GRN, CRM)
Dragon Shirt @ $5.00			
Dragon Chef's Apron @ $10.00			
		Total enclosed $ _____	

· ·

Mail to:

BARD HALL PRESS
32 Knickerbocker Road
Tenafly, New Jersey 07670

Notes